LEARNING RIGHT FROM ~~WONG~~, ~~WRONG~~, ~~WOKE~~, LEFT

CHRIS 'BILKO' STOKES

BALBOA.PRESS
A DIVISION OF HAY HOUSE

Copyright © 2020 Chris 'Bilko' Stokes.

All rights reserved. No part of this book may be used or reproduced by any means, graphic, electronic, or mechanical, including photocopying, recording, taping or by any information storage retrieval system without the written permission of the author except in the case of brief quotations embodied in critical articles and reviews.

Balboa Press books may be ordered through booksellers or by contacting:

Balboa Press
A Division of Hay House
1663 Liberty Drive
Bloomington, IN 47403
www.balboapress.com.au
AU TFN: 1 800 844 925 (Toll Free inside Australia)
AU Local: 0283 107 086 (+61 2 8310 7086 from outside Australia)

Because of the dynamic nature of the Internet, any web addresses or links contained in this book may have changed since publication and may no longer be valid. The views expressed in this work are solely those of the author and do not necessarily reflect the views of the publisher, and the publisher hereby disclaims any responsibility for them.

The author of this book does not dispense medical advice or prescribe the use of any technique as a form of treatment for physical, emotional, or medical problems without the advice of a physician, either directly or indirectly. The intent of the author is only to offer information of a general nature to help you in your quest for emotional and spiritual well-being. In the event you use any of the information in this book for yourself, which is your constitutional right, the author and the publisher assume no responsibility for your actions.

Any people depicted in stock imagery provided by Getty Images are models, and such images are being used for illustrative purposes only. Certain stock imagery © Getty Images.

Print information available on the last page.

ISBN: 978-1-5043-2200-3 (sc)
ISBN: 978-1-5043-2215-7 (e)

Balboa Press rev. date: 10/16/2020

Contents

Acknowledgement ix
Preface/Foreword xi
Introduction xiii

1 The Last Century 1
1.1 Rampant technological intervention 1
1.2 The growth of the super powers 3
1.3 The rise of China 8
1.4 The virtues of capitalism 9
1.5 Growing disparity despite regional independence 11
1.6 The status quo 11

2 Western Expansion Through Capitalism 15
2.1 The importance of history 15
2.2 The greatest lessons 18
2.3 Control the skies 18
2.4 Communication lessons 20
2.5 Control the seas 21
2.6 Let sleeping dogs lie 24
2.7 The increasing power of scientists 26

3 When Simplicity Gives Way to Complexity 28
3.1 Learning 28
3.2 Right 29
3.3 From 30
3.4 Wong 31
3.5 Wrong 32
3.6 Woke 33
3.7 Left 36

4　The Political Combatants 38
4.1 Throwing fuel on the fire 38
4.2 The modern dilemma 44
4.3 The right capitalists 46
4.4 The Socialist left 48
4.5 The greens and independents 51
4.6 One Nation Party 53

5　Conflict Within the "Five Eyes." 56
5.1 Globalisation unifies the battle 56
5.2 The Republicans step up in the USA 62
5.3 The United Kingdom steps back from Europe 63
5.4 The quiet Aussies speak up down under 68
5.5 Canada squeezes the life out of the left 76
5.6 The conservatives retain plurality in New Zealand 77

6　The Rising Threat of Socialism 80
6.1 A sense of inevitability? 80
6.2 Marxism 81
6.3 The hurdle confronting the left 84
6.4 Two peas in a pod 86
6.5 The rise of the mob 90

7　Understanding Humanity 93
7.1 Knowing the opposition 93
7.2 Anatomy 94
7.3 Behaviour 99
7.4 Conditioning 101
7.5 Control 104
7.6 Narcissism, the socialist mecca 107
7.7 Trust and respect 108
7.8 Rewriting history 113
7.9 The decline of religion 119
7.10 Devaluing science 121

8 The Three Trojan Horses **124**
8.1 Which straw will break the camel's back? 124
8.2 The global warming hoax 125
8.3 Covid-19, the great leveller 133
8.4 Antifa emerges from the shadows 142

9 Navigating the Point of No Return **151**
9.1 Light your own fire 151
9.2 Forthcoming resilience of the right 153
9.3 Bias, hypocrisy, racism and lies 165
9.4 Wokeness, the Achilles heel of the socialists 181
9.5 Every cloud has a silver lining 185
9.6 All is not lost 192

Epilogue 203

Acknowledgement

I would just like to thank my wife and children, for supporting me through my condition, and having the patience to bear with me, as I compiled the information contained in this book. The restless, sleepless nights are now hopefully behind us. Special thanks too, to my mum for her contribution of witty sayings that permeate this book. Thanks too, must go to the illustrator of the book cover. Finally, thank you to the readers who take the time to read this. We could all do with a little enlightenment.

Preface/Foreword

What a crazy world in which we live. Never has there been so much change and seemingly, in so little time. In fact, before the very eyes of one generation. Having hit the golden fifty years of age I was struck by how quickly time has flown, and whether I have given life my all. I have always been a bloke who grabbed life with both hands. I lived by the creed that, "if you are not living on the edge, you are taking up too much space." It served me well. Completing a degree (majoring in economic geography at the Uni of New South Wales and also a trade (becoming a fully-licensed plumber), I have enriched myself with a wonderful education, and worked hard to attain a comfortable life.

I have enjoyed moderate sporting success at an amateur level, but more importantly, fully embraced my local community through running, cricket, rugby league, and surf boat rowing (all staples of Australian society). I have been fortunate to get married, and raise three wonderful children, who are now the inspiration to put pen to paper. In Sydney, and in this day and age, I consider myself most fortunate.

The son of a pair of "ten-pound poms" who emigrated in the late 1960's from mother England, I am the only Aussie in my whole family tree. How lucky am I? To be raised and now reside in Sydney, only accentuates this further. To quote an old boatie mate, "first, we were winning, then we were swimming." (love your work Termite!) Alas my world began to crumble. Unfortunately, I suffered a career-ending injury while "on the tools" as a plumber. Whilst it put an end to a moderately lucrative and rewarding career, it did open my eyes, as to what the heck is really going on in this world.

Thrust into the world of ongoing medical treatment and insurance litigation, I began to see the world without looking through a pair of rose-coloured glasses. Five hundred-odd, medical and legal appointments later, I am still afflicted and severely inconvenienced by injuries sustained at work. Mentally scarred by the "bullshit corruption" of conflicting doctors and insurance company representatives, I saw a light shining at the end of the tunnel. If we are not careful though, this light will be switched off due to a recession!

Whilst my condition is progressive and incurable, it has given me time to evaluate what is really important in this world. That is undoubtedly, the health and wealth of myself, my wife, our three kids and the general population at large. The sole purpose of this book is to enlighten my children, our youth, and their parents, about the corruption and coercion playing out before our eyes amongst the main combatants… the media, politicians, and tyrannical technocrats. This phenomenon has given rise to the greatest threat that humanity has known. "Socialism" is again rising from the ashes.

I write this book to hopefully raise further awareness of these issues playing out before our very eyes. A simple, concise summary of where we have been, how we got here, but most importantly, how society is teetering on the edge of a precipice. By all means, one has to "light your own fire," to fully embrace all that life has to offer. But, collectively, we also have the power to either destabilize society or to restore order and maintain international peace.

Make you own decisions in life and learn from your mistakes, but most importantly, hang on for the ride and enjoy it. Afterall, "you only live once." To do this freely, one needs to pay attention to the ever-changing political landscape because we all have a say in how our nation is forged and shaped. Our very survival may one day depend on it. Happy reading… and happy voting.

Introduction

Whether it be fake news, corrupt politicians, collapsing economies, pandemics, religious and cultural wars, natural disasters or the dreaded climate change, all these dilemmas are now playing out at once and competing for your attention. They are disturbingly and quietly, dividing personal opinions, communities, and nations alike.

Our children, graduating from schools at the ripe old age of seventeen or eighteen, are being fought over as a means of furthering biased causes, agendas, and political strength. Like seagulls scrapping over a strewn handful of soggy hot chips at the beach on a balmy, blustery day, our leaders are preying on our vulnerable young. They are selfishly doing this when our kids are at an impressionable age.

At eighteen years of age, our children are old enough to go to the pub and get smashed (drunk as the older generation used to call it), if they so wish. They are old enough to drive a vehicle unaccompanied, once they have attained their driving license. They are also old enough to vote. This is where the battlelines are being drawn in the sand. Whether it be a leaning towards a labour, liberal, green, republican, conservative, progressive, democrat or independent political allegiance, the fight is on in earnest for our children's minds and most importantly, their vote.

But what are they being taught? Do we value it? Do we trust our current teachers, education ministers, media outlets, social forums, and ruling governments to give our children an unbiased, objective education? Do we ready them to enter the workforce with a balanced, realistic view of the world and its intricate workings? Or have we, as teachers, parents, and adults, become so consumed in our own little world, that we have taken our eyes off the ball and wrongly assumed that our elected governments will make sure things are ok?

Society cannot survive for very long, if our young are being taught to hate it. Growing inequality, uprisings in radical behaviour, and social media chatter are creating concern that lessons of the past are being quickly forgotten.

The musings and utterings of my own children, and the dribble that plays out on social mediums, suggests that corruption and bias are rampant, and worsening at an alarming rate. So much so, that our education system is in need of an overhaul. We are sent off to school to learn primarily about literacy and numeracy, and also develop the all-important social skills necessary to navigate life.

We are taught good manners very early on, and then we quickly learn our left hands and feet from our right. Then, as we get older, little attention has been paid to learning the difference between "right and wong … err wrong… err woke… err left." That is, objectively developing our own political beliefs and aversions. The current state of affairs of the world, is highlighting the urgent need for a re-evaluation and rethink. The politicisation and weaponization of just about everything are the new norm.

In a hard, fast-paced world, our education standards are slipping. Australia is sliding down the list of countries ranked on their numeracy and literacy skills. It stands to reason then, that other facets of education such as history, science, and the arts are also in decline, as our secondary schools ready our graduating students for a world full of technology, computers and opportunities.

Alas, the big, fast world has also never been more unforgiving, with rising inequality among individuals, corporations and countries. National debt levels across the globe, are rising to astronomical levels. The greed that propelled this rapid advancement in development, has also manifested itself in a ruthless quest to become the most powerful.

I am quite sure, none of this is being discussed in classrooms. If it does pop up in conversations, I have serious doubts as to whether the merits and problems with this, are being argued vigorously. "We don't have time as we are flat out, just getting through the set curriculum," say the teachers. But who sets the curriculum, and what is in it these days?

It is time to awaken our youth and their parents to what is really at stake. In a time-poor society, our youth are too busy trying to finish their studies, find employment, build relationships, stay fit, look cool, and get ahead. Very few of them seriously give politics a second thought. They rarely show an interest in current affairs of the day and prefer social media, music, and videos over talkback radio and news-based television. Likewise, parents are also often too busy to instil in their offspring, an understanding of the two sides of the political spectrum and the myriad of off-shoot political systems.

It is time "a few home truths" were told. Our young are being conditioned to take sides, and their views of the world are being distorted by media bias. We are now seeing significant social unrest, as socialists and activists, seek to destabilise governments and overthrow capitalism. Whatever happened to the old adage "to win with dignity or lose with grace?"

What has caused this, and what can be done about it?

1
The Last Century

1.1 Rampant technological intervention

What we see today, in terms of socioeconomic forces, has been playing out for hundreds of years. The rise and fall of countries, economies, and governments has had an almost cyclical nature. But the twenty-first century has bought so much change through advances in technology and communications, that it could be said that "the world is on steroids." It has got too big and fast for its own good, whilst also becoming unstable. Look back over the years and it is easy to see why.

Our current generation of school leavers, university graduates, and young men and women, are living through the most rapid technological advances in the history of mankind. The industrial revolution of last century, would appear to have evolved in slow motion in comparison to what we see today.

Ever since man abandoned the old "horse and cart" and got into the automobile, life seems to have sped up. Everything became closer in real terms. History seems to have been made and recorded in an abbreviated fashion. Monumental, life-changing advances in technology, medicine, construction, communication, and social development, quickly become yesterday's news. Likewise, herculean cultural and sporting human endeavours and achievements, are harshly and quickly confined to the dustbin of yesteryear.

Good, old-fashioned record books (listing historical human achievements), are now seen as little more than dust collectors, uselessly littering libraries and book shelves. Any perceived relevant information therein, is nowadays, stored alternately on a disc or uploaded to the internet. "Out of sight, out of mind." Libraries are actually shrinking as old hard copies of books are replaced by electronic records, microfiche, discs, and computer hardware and software. But, is this new means of storing data being compiled accurately and objectively?

"Humankind" (today's politically correct word for us all, now used instead of the simpler, more pronounceable mankind) developed an insatiable appetite for wanting more, and wanting it quicker. We have become the greatest generation of consumers in the recorded history of the planet. Our thirst and hunger for technology and wealth has increased almost exponentially.

Some would say we have "inadvertently" nurtured greed in an unfathomable, irreversible, and somewhat regrettable fashion. Unfortunately, these people also, often do not want to be seen or heard saying it. Hence, the rise too, of the "keyboard warrior" which I shall touch on later.

Having endured two World Wars and the great depressions, mankind was suddenly invincible. The roaring twenties, after World War One, was a golden time for happiness, wealth, and general prosperity. With the misery of war, famine, and death behind us, population numbers soon were on the rise. Social interaction multiplied, and it once again became safe and popular to bring children into the world.

Work opportunities became abundant, and with the growth of industry, wealth increased rapidly among industrialised nations, thereby substantially improving our quality of life. Combined with medical advances (advent of penicillin and eradication of a few diseases that had plagued the planet), we were now living much longer, as society soon left the social unrest and economic "gloom and doom" behind.

Entrepreneurs saw opportunity and quickly latched onto it. The means of communication multiplied (print media, telephone, wireless, and television), and technological advances gave rise to greater productivity through automation in the manufacturing sector. Soon, greater freight carrying capacity across land (rail) and oceans (super tankers/container ships), enabled new markets in countries far away to be accessed. The pronounced development in communications, and the growing emphasis on marketing and advertising, were creating a whole new range of opportunities for the populace.

Just like with the advent of cars, everyone had been bought closer together, and the "speed of life" was seemingly on the rise as the years flew by. There were never enough hours in the day. All of a sudden, there was a serious dollar to be made. Amongst this backdrop, education standards were on the increase. Society throughout this, despite being more affluent, had clearly learnt from the past, but never forgot where its origins lay. Religions of all denomination and national pride, continued to flourish, as the world had become a harmonious little community.

The one exception to all this, was in the Eastern Bloc. The United Soviet Socialist Republic (USSR), was flirting with socialism after World War One. Along with Germany and then Italy, these regions began to take on a communist political aversion. However, they were proving to be unstable in comparison to the West. Created wealth was not being distributed evenly in these countries, which was to have an important bearing on world stability a few years later. Socialist forces were at play in these regions, which were to have a destabilising effect on the rest of Europe.

1.2 The growth of the super powers

Conversely, out of this rise in ensuing wealth, powerful nations began to emerge. The United States of America, The United Soviet Socialist Republic, France, The United Kingdom, Germany, and Australia amongst others, had undergone rampant urbanisation and economic development, to earn their current status as First World countries. Western nations of the civilised world, were benefitting from trade and shared in rapid economic growth.

On the other side of the planet, many Asian and African countries were geographically isolated in harsh climates, and also had rapidly exploding populations which diminished their average living standards. Economic growth levels varied from region to region.

Gross Domestic Product (GDP) in these Asian countries was lower than that of the wealthier First World nations. Health and education standards too, lagged behind for these economically disadvantaged countries. Combined with drought, natural disasters, and political instability, they fell further behind the rest of the world in economic terms, as they were ravaged by local war and famine. The inevitable political instability, (usually the result of unequal wealth redistribution, combined with religious or cultural conflict) gave rise to civil disobedience and social unrest in many of these regions.

In the 1960's and 1970's, the spectre of war was again upon us. The late sixties saw the Vietnam War, where The United States of America (USA) and its allies intervened, in order to keep the peace. Enormous casualties were sustained, as the West sought a suitable means of ending the war in Cambodia and Vietnam. Religious fervour was also at the heart of ongoing conflict amongst the Middle East countries and indeed, continues to this very day.

Elsewhere, tension between North and South Korea has had a marked effect on the population and living standards of both nations. Differing political systems have given rise to tensions along their border for decades.

Pakistan and India had massive populations developing their economies, but this only seemed to hinder their ability to catch up to the Western world (in per capita terms). They were soon left behind economically. As far as the rest of world was concerned, these two nations were preoccupied with annoying each other in border skirmishes, as they fought for control of the land in the adjoining Kashmir region.

The 1960's and 1970's both flew by quickly, as advances in the media and music industries saw another big wealth multiplier created. Solo music artists and bands shot to stardom, often becoming world-famous thanks to the radio and then television. Rapid growth in the sale of vinyl records, audio cassettes, and then Compact Discs and Videos, saw the wealth of prominent artists reach astronomical proportions. The talent, music, and dancing of these artists, saw them marketable to worldwide audiences. The dollars flowed, and soon the world was "as one," listening to the same music, as these artists toured the world to play before their adoring fans. It seemed "globalisation" was becoming the new norm.

The 1980's, saw the brief conflict between Argentina and the United Kingdom over the Falkland Islands. World leaders became nervous that this may escalate, but resolute military action by the British bought a quick end to this war. It seems looking back though, that rumblings of discontent were starting to "rear their ugly heads." In the grand scheme of things, this was little more than a battle for a strategic island. Sovereign control of the Falkland Islands was an economic and military benefit to the United Kingdom.

Globalisation has been aided and abetted by further advances in communication. This increased trade, and thus created whole new markets for resources, products and knowledge. The "space race" between America and Russia saw the last frontier of space conquered. Apart from "putting man on the moon," we have successfully deployed numerous satellites into orbit. The relay of signals, meant that the rest of the world was now at our fingertips. Local news was soon making way for international current affairs. Things were happening fast. Opportunities and new markets were now within reach. Never was so much money being made, by so many.

Economic analysis took on new meaning. The success of an individual, family, corporation, or country was quickly gauged by looking at the economic figures of the entity. Profit and loss statements,

Gross Domestic Product (GDP) figures, budgets, forecasts, growth forecasts, and market share, became key performance indicators (KPI's) in business circles and amongst elected government officials.

The emerging superpowers were now even more determined to grow their market share and keep themselves financially ahead of their counterparts. During the 1980's, factional infighting amongst the states of the USSR saw it destabilised, as the ruling government sought to retain control of its borders. This destabilisation saw it lose equal billing, with the United States, as the greatest super power.

Victorious, traditional allies from World War Two had traded among themselves successfully, but were now eager to engage with the rest of the world. Soon, America had gained the ascendancy and is now considered the world's leading super power. But, despite this amicable importing and exporting between nations, there was still an underlying suspicion of one another, and there always will be.

Even today, this rational human behaviour can be seen in enterprises such as Coca Cola, which guards its secret ingredient recipe from competitors such as Pepsi. Preserving profit was a primary goal for individuals, companies, and countries alike. After all, the health, safety, wellbeing, and defence of individuals and nations, was still paramount in respective country agendas. But these all require wealth to finance them.

Trade enabled many regions to prosper, but history has always shown, that eventually disparity and inequality will inevitably soon develop, often leading firstly, to social unease and then finally to conflict. The race was and still is on. Economic growth had created wealth, strength and power, but had also become an integral part of the "human psyche," as we adopted a "more, better, best" mentality to just about everything. With larger revenue, governments began to place a greater emphasis on defence, nationalism, and research. Before we knew it, countries were spending enormous amounts of money on expanding their military might.

Unimaginable technological advances saw the creation of massive naval fleets, upgraded air forces, advanced weaponry, and military training. Radar, submarines, the proliferation of nuclear arms, and espionage, had all increased the power, reach, stealth, and ultimately, the strength of nations. With this, came an uneasiness and collective fear of the stockpile of weaponry that had been amassed worldwide.

During the twenty-first century, the USA had gained the unofficial title of the "world police." The United States military strength is regarded as "second to none." This was never more evident, than during the liberation of Kuwait from Iraqi occupation during the first Gulf War. America had stepped in to liberate the people of Kuwait who were invaded by Iraq. Or so it seemed. Were the Americans also keeping their crude oil supply lines open to service their thriving economy?

The USA was again to the rescue, when Saddam Hussein of Iraq, began threatening the world with his supposed "weapons of mass destruction." He was later terminated. Iraq was freed of tyranny, and a new government was installed to this warring nation, to assist in restoring democracy to its long-suffering people.

America, like Russia before it, now finds it has military forces stranded in Afghanistan, which cannot be withdrawn confidently without destabilizing existing levels of peace. Rather than fighting a war, American forces today remain in the Middle East, as a first line of defence against terrorism.

Terrorism has reared its ugly head in the last twenty years. The 9/11 attacks in New York, ongoing tension in the Middle East, conflict in Syria, and the rise of ISIS (Islamic State), have left the world in a fragile state. The seemingly, endless battle of fighting for freedom, has come at a heavy cost. The people of the Western world appear battle weary at the ongoing loss of life and the increased budgetary demands to maintain military strength. They have grown tired of the losses with no apparent gains. Has this fatigue softened the will of the people to confront local issues that "are now rearing their ugly head?"

The will to fight appears to have subsided. World debt levels have soared to new highs. It seems that this rapid economic growth, through advances in technology since the end of World War Two, has left us breathless and in need of time to catch our breath. But no. The break-neck speed of life has left us addicted to material possession and wealth creation. "No work no play" is the creed. As a species we have become conditioned to wanting more money, and ultimately the power, independence, and freedom, that come with it.

1.3 The rise of China

Most significantly amongst all this, China and its burgeoning population, was quietly minding its own business. Given that it was under communist rule, it seemed that the West had, for the large part, ignored it. China appeared to be economically behind the rest of the world. The communist political system, whereby the Chinese State had all ownership and distributed wealth according to contribution and need, had long been renounced as a "flawed concept."

Censorship of the inhabitants and geographic isolation, had constricted the Chinese economy, while Western society had concerns trading with the People's Republic of China. History had previously shown that communist regimes were always doomed to misery, mired in controversy, and were a gross deterrent on freedom. Conformity with the ruling party agenda, meant harsh penalties for non-compliance, and soon China was stigmatised for having a poor human rights record.

Alarmed at their massive population projections, in the 1970's and 1980's, the Chinese Communist Party implemented social engineering, which culminated in a "one child policy" designed to curb its population numbers. Unfortunately, history has shown that the Chinese are also a very proud race who traditionally, seek to preserve their family name. A lot of families chose to abort female offspring and only keep their first-born child if it were a male. Fast forward twenty-five years, and all of a sudden you have a predominantly male population and the significant man power, to field the greatest cavalry in the world's history. How significant will this be, in years to come?

Likewise, with a vast labour force, wages were low and China soon began to manufacture goods for a growing world population. With cheaper labour costs, they were soon entering the international market, flooding it with cheaper goods, though often of inferior quality. None the less, is was becoming a major player by world standards. The nation under communist rule, was eager to access the wealth excesses of the West.

While China was on the march, the nuclear arms race had seen the "Cold War" between the USSR and the USA inject fear to the wider community. Diplomacy, thankfully, saw tensions ease and the world went on about its business. Following this, man was increasingly becoming obsessed with the best way to grow "the economic pie," whilst seemingly, being too busy and preoccupied to ensure an equitable distribution of wealth among the population. Opposing political parties were starting to contest with vigour, both the means to improve economic growth, and also the means with which to distribute the wealth created.

1.4 The virtues of capitalism

Capitalism, whereby economic growth and wealth is mainly derived and shared by private and individual entities, was rising and everyone it seemed, wanted to "ride this gravy train." Governments collected significant revenue through the taxation of profits, and this has been successfully redistributed through the welfare system. It has seemingly guided the world to greater riches and improved the "quality of life" for those who want it.

Gross Domestic Product (GDP) became the flag bearer for all sovereign nations, and testimony to a region or country's respective wealth. Seldom would an hourly news report or daily news bulletin pass, without some reporting of current economic figures. As the technological and communication advances spread, so too, did awareness of the growing divide in wealth amongst nations previously considered "Third World."

Often, leaders of poorer nations would "covet" the wealth of the West, and this would lead to internal divisions. Corruption in poorer nations, saw untold wealth accumulated by the elite rulers, while the rest of the population lived "below" the poverty line. Factions often formed along religious differences, and battles for power developed within these poorer regions. Internal conflicts and tension along borders, often required peace-keeping forces supplied by leading Western nations.

Air and space travel (precipitating the deployment of advanced satellites), allowed knowledge and wealth to spread around the globe in record fashion. Overnight seemingly, the world had become a "global village." As a finite market, the nations of the world were eager to have the greatest share of customers. The stock markets became accessible worldwide, and soon became another means to acquire or lose economic fortunes.

The United States of America, with its superpower military strength, quickly became the economic juggernaut of our generation. Its old adversary, the United Soviet Socialist Republic (USSR), was and still is, also seeking to show its might by dominating the European region in military strength, if not economic prowess. The United Kingdom joined up with other European nations to form their own European Union, complete with its own currency; the Euro Dollar.

The historically troubled Middle East countries, continued to suffer political and social unrest, usually concerning religious and cultural differences. Underlying this geographical region though, is an abundance of oil, the natural resource which has been extracted and refined to quell the insatiable economic thirst of the Western world. It too, has bought untold wealth to a politically unstable region.

Alas, it would be fair to say, that this wealth has clearly not been shared equally among the region's habitants. There is a growing social and political unrest over the inequity of the health and wealth of the populace. Religion and ethnicity are where the battle lines are drawn for the combatants of the Middle East, but look below the surface, and it's clear that the quest for wealth and power is all-consuming.

1.5 Growing disparity despite regional independence

Meanwhile, the South American countries, as well as Africa, Indonesia, South Africa, Canada, Australia, and New Zealand, have all been beneficiaries of this growth through technological advancement. Trade of respective natural resources, manufactured products, and tourism, have opened up new markets for these countries. As each country extracted its natural resources for economic means, the world was becoming a safer, more prosperous place. Greater cooperation, reliance, and dependence upon one another, was soon assumed, as economies continued to thrive and populations began to swell.

All the while, the relatively distant Asian countries were quietly going about their own business. Japan, Taiwan, Vietnam, Singapore, North and South Korea, and China, (all with differing social and political ideologies), were seem as "untapped potential" in a region far away from prying eyes. They were the last bastion in previously ignored markets. Trade between these competing nations was soon quickly expanded, virtually overnight.

Everyone "wanted in" on economic growth. But depending on your population size, ethnic composition, and skill of your workforce, not every country was faring as well as the leading Western nations.

1.6 The status quo

Before we knew it, we were driving German or Japanese cars, wearing clothes and shoes made in China, watching television on screens made in Japan, or were holidaying in Vietnam. But no one seemed to care.

We were all having too much fun and "took our eyes off the ball." We are working longer and harder to finance it all, but it's a battle we are now struggling to win, as debt at private and national levels, is spiralling out of control.

Travel and communication have opened up sporting markets like never before. The humble sport of cricket seemingly opened up Pakistan, Sri Lanka, and India. These are proving to be massive markets, which are being exploited by competitors, marketing companies, betting agencies, and broadcasting corporations.

Indeed, it seems you cannot walk any street in the world, without seeing an English Premier League soccer jersey being worn by the local kids on the street. We can all admit to having previously watched some documentary about underprivileged regions, and seen a little kid kicking a crappy old soccer ball, while adorned in an Arsenal, Liverpool, or Barcelona jersey; and with "Messi" or "Ronaldo" plastered on the back.

The advent of mobile phones, the internet (World Wide Web), and the whole "dot.com" explosion at the start of the twenty-first century, put this technology-driven word into overspeed. It seems in the "blink of an eye," or most certainly in one generation, we have been caught up in a time warp of our own making. "The years roll by" ever too quickly as it is. We often hear our parents or grandparents as they encourage us to "enjoy our youth" which disappears all too quickly. Time waits for no man. This tech-savvy world seems to be running on fast-forward.

Turn on your television today (the latest, biggest, trendy, flat screen LCD or plasma model), log on to your computer, flip open your lap top, or reach for your mobile phone, and the picture is the same. Before you can change the channel, search the internet for your query, check out your missed calls and messages, or "suss out" the latest in tweets and memes, you have already been bombarded. In front of you is a kaleidoscope of mesmerising, eye-catching, colourful displays, and seemingly worthless advertising. Embedded in this, dare I say it, is "subliminal propaganda and messaging." All diligently engineered by todays' Information Technology experts (IT). All too, designed to capture a market for some clever enterprise or political party.

Look beneath the veneer of expanding economic growth and the rise in world stock markets, and you will see the greatest threat known to mankind. The "battle" for our minds. It is this fierce subliminal contest, that has the potential to undo all the growth and development attained since the 1940's.

Economic growth has become a stepping stone to power. Just like the previous wars fought over land and wealth. We are in the midst of a war to end all wars. "Control of the people" is the ultimate means to attaining power and gaining control of the wealth.

It is an intrusive, yet covert, war borne out of technological advancement, that is being fought more willingly, than all that have gone before. It can honestly "take away your breath" with the fantastic graphics, up-to-date information, and access at your fingertips. Before you know it, you cannot help the urge to be driving a motor vehicle and phoning or texting someone while you drive. That is how crazy and obsessed we have become. Fortunately, the law is catching up on this past time, with heavy fines now imposed. For some though, it's still not a deterrent! That's right! We are risking our lives in our obsession with technology that knows no bounds.

You can see this again, when it comes to pedestrian safety. People are now in a trance walking down the footpath, face glued to their mobile phone screens. Worse still, their sense of hearing is "out with the washing" too, as they listen to the "latest sounds on their air pods." How many times do you see people bump into one another or step into oncoming traffic? Even worse, you get a "dirty look" if you interrupt their concentration.

This digital age is also on the verge of giving us a cashless society. God only knows what this will do for our economies. Opinions are divided on this, but I know that old folk haven't been able to keep up with technology, and will no doubt struggle. Recent health concerns over the dirtiness of physical currency, may expedite this transition to digital currency. One can only expect cryptocurrency, cyber-attacks, and on-line scams, to threaten this potential transition in the digital age.

Look beneath the veneer of expanding economic growth and the rise in world stock markets. Ignore for a moment, the incessant daily reports about the "Dow Jones index," or the "all ordinaries," or the status of the local stock market and exchange rate. Look and listen closely to the news, advertising from the various media outlets, Facebook, and other social mediums, and you can see an ugly, concerning phenomenon is taking place.

Whilst we have allowed ourselves to indulge in the comforts and financial security that knowledge and technology have bought us, our complacency has seen us take our eyes off another important agenda. Our health, safety, and wellbeing, has been put at stake by this rampant obsession with growing the economic pie. Individuals, companies, and whole nations, have put profit before people. Some are highly successful. Others have gone bankrupt, ruining people's lives in the process. With the wealth, is where "the power resides."

There is a growing disparity between the "haves" and the "have nots." Wealth distribution has recently, never been so uneven. It has given rise to tensions between individuals, companies, and most worryingly, whole nations.

Unfortunately, every news article or media report, now also seems to come with subjective overtones. Gone are the journalistic "golden days" of honest, objective facts and stories being reported accurately. Again, in the modern world, there is a "dollar to be made" with the speed of news reporting. Coupled with this, is the politicisation and weaponization of the news, advertising, and indeed, all social platforms.

2

Western Expansion Through Capitalism

2.1 The importance of history

"You will not know where you are heading, if you haven't paid attention to where you are coming from." Never a more apt truism. Yet in this modern world, the study of history, the arts, literature, and politics, are seen as boring, yesterday's subjects, and irrelevant to where the youth of today want to be heading.

This is perilous as our population ages. The problems this will present, are compounded, when you factor in today's speed of life. Our parents and guardians are so time-poor, that they overlook the need to offer advice to their children about mainstream societal and political issues.

When you consider the state of society at present, history has never been more important. Consider what forces are trying to destabilise governments of the Western world, and their respective motives. George Orwell (author of the political masterpiece "1984"), back in 1949, wrote "who controls the past controls the future. Who controls the present, controls the past!" Consider this, when you look at recent election results, the success of capitalism, and leftist efforts to change the course of history by removing all records of the past.

Couple this, with the disinterest our youth have, in reading the newspapers, listening to talk-back radio, watching current affairs or watching topical current affairs discussions on channels such as the ABC, BBC, CNN, MSNBC or those on Sky News (News Corp).

We have become so complacent in this generation, that we have falsely assumed that our children's educational needs are broadly being met at secondary school and at universities. These used to be the last bastion of free-thinking higher education, but not anymore. Also pay close attention to the social mediums. You will notice a growing groundswell of discontent, and mounting, outright concern, at the lack of objective information being delivered to our youth and students, as part of their secondary or tertiary education.

There is a major political bias in our education system skewed heavily to the left. Our youth are being brainwashed and no one is speaking up to point this out. Those that try are shouted down. There is an air of intimidation about society. Intelligent, quiet folk can see it but are too afraid to speak their mind, voice their opinion, or write down and express their thoughts. The time has come for this ethos to change.

Worse still, is that elected leaders and politicians, are too reticent to correct this growing problem. They are more concerned with being seen as politically correct, than in actually resolving problems through effective policy. In years to come, this will manifest itself in the voting patterns of our future electorate. This growing imbalance in what is being taught, is quickly eroding all the wealth and gains accrued by those living during the last sixty years. Everything we have gained in this mad technological march, is being frittered away through a culture war that has now engulfed Western civilisations.

At the heart of this culture war is "wokeness." This "increased level of awareness about inequality" has invaded every discussion, writing, news article, television story, and mandated law. It has become so powerful, that it has direct influence over everything we see, do or hear.

Wokeness has caused us to "lose sight of the bigger picture." It seems that every action or any words spoken by any politician, famous television personality star, athlete or person of note, are quickly ridiculed or debated in public; be it on television, on the radio, on Facebook or in the Twittersphere.

In recent times, it has created a cancel culture so intimidating, that businesses or enterprises are duped and coerced into changing the name and appearance of their branding just because it might somehow offend somebody.

All the while, China has begun to assert its authority in the South Pacific. What was once a quiet country with its own internal squabbling, has quickly become a major threat to world markets, peace, and stability. This quiet communist country has awoken from its slumber. It has thrust itself onto the world stage, in order to compete with the United States of America for global supremacy.

History has seen a similar rise once before. In 1939, twenty-odd years after the end of World War One, Germany under the tyrannical Dictatorship of Adolf Hitler, had rose to power. His totalitarian regime had converted Germany to a system of national socialism. Quickly, it had amassed an enormous armed force and began strangling the economic life out of Europe.

Hitler was a fanatical nut, consumed by the desire to create a superior race of human being. World domination was his end goal. To the ultimate horror of the free world, he began an ethnic cleansing of the Jewish people in his own country. As his power grew, his armed forces invaded Poland and other neighbouring countries. World War Two had begun, as the Western allies united in combat, to confront this growing threat. Years later, this war was fought out in just about every corner of the planet. The battle was on. The prize? Freedom!

2.2 The greatest lessons

The greatest lessons to be learnt from World War Two were the manner in which it was fought, and how it was eventually won. "Necessity is the mother of invention." Every country was researching more effective means to combat the enemy. Secrecy surrounding technological advances, was improving the ability to fight the enemy, and to defend sovereign territory. The desire to defend, maintain or increase power, saw rapid advances in the means of fighting during this conflict.

Afterall, the number one goal of every government is to "protect its own people." When neighbouring countries get invaded, your enemy can be on your doorstep, hence the need to form alliances to protect your own sovereignty from afar. Once you can defend your borders, then you can protect you own people within, through effective law and order.

Allies from yesteryear, are still friends and co-operative today, while suspicions still abound about defeated enemies. All the while, many technological advances derived during the war years, are still with us today. War proved to be a generator of national wealth. For example, production of ordinance and weaponry created industries which improved overall economic wellbeing. Telecommunications systems were crude in yesteryear, but they were a forebearer to the rapid growth experienced in this industry today.

2.3 Control the skies

Early dominance of the air during the 1930's, was by the use of giant airships. The first controlled and manned air flights were the in Zeppelins, at the turn of the twentieth century, by the Germans. These put fear into the Europeans, as they could destroy cities by dropping bombs from above. They were also used for forward reconnaissance, giving an advantage to invading armies. However, they were slow and cumbersome, and an easy target for enemy fire. As such their success was short-lived. But they paved the way for military success to be achieved in the skies above.

Land-based invasions of neighbouring territories were relatively straight forward, with ground forces consisting of armoured vehicles and heavy infantry armadas. These usually followed an aerial bombardment, consisting of relatively light ordinance (small bombs dropped from short range aircraft) blitzes on enemy positions.

The use of aircraft to initiate attacks, was effective in softening enemy defences. This helped to minimise casualties on the ground, as infantry advanced on opposition territory. Apart from being used to drop bombs, alternately, a supply of ammunition, first aid, and food, could be quickly delivered to your front line of troops. This helped to gain and hold territory, until the main armed forces arrived thereafter.

As German forces advanced through Europe, they knew that to ultimately succeed, they had to invade and occupy the United Kingdom. Whilst the Germans ultimately failed in this conquest, it was the use of the "spitfire" aircraft by the British, that saw the battle being won in the skies. The Germans had begun "saturation" bombing London to soften up the enemy. The cumbersome, heavy German bombers were no match for the agile and smaller, but much faster, defensive fighting aircraft of the British Airforce. It was a lesson not forgotten, as even today, economic growth is enhanced by controlling the flow of goods, wealth, and means of communication, through the skies of planet earth.

For Hitler's plan of "ruling the world" to succeed, he had to invade, then occupy and finally retain, control of occupied nations. Germany garnered support from its own axis-powers, as Italy and Japan joined the fight against the allies. Japan had its own territorial war with China, whilst Hitler was on the march. It seemed that the whole world had taken two sides.

This was a battle about ideology, as much as it was for territory. There were two sides. The allies were for freedom and democracy, whilst the axis powers were ruled in a socialist, communist manner. It pays to remember this poignant feature, when trying to understand the issues we all confront today.

2.4 Communication lessons

Another key lesson in this great war, was the importance of communication. The key to united battlefront wins, was the coordination of armed forces from different countries. The greatest day in armed history occurred on June 6, 1945. Better known as "D-Day." By then, America had been drawn into the war after Japan had attacked Pearl Harbour in 1941. The Allied forces had amassed the greatest Armada (naval fleet) known in warfare history.

After limited aerial bombing of German bunkers on the beaches of Normandy, France, a flotilla of Allied naval and civilian craft assembled at sea in the English Channel, carrying British, American and Australian soldiers. The plan to drive German forces back out of France and Europe had begun. Allied forces stormed the beach in record numbers and despite incurring heavy casualties, regained control of the beach from the Germans. The battle to drive Hitler's occupying forces back to Berlin "was on in earnest."

Apart from the sheer size and scale of the amassed sea Armada, the ultimate success was down to the planning and communication of the Allies. Advances in meteorology, mapping, secret radio telegraphs and the use of Morse code, allowed for the synchronized attack at Normandy, which marked the beginning of the end for German occupation of Europe.

Today, warfare is conducted by computer technology. Smart bombs and guided missiles, using radar or GPS (Global Positioning Satellites), prove a reliable deterrent to the enemy. The importance of communication, and lessons from previous wars have been learnt. A lesson too, had been learnt in the most effective means to conduct warfare. Before any attack or invasion, an armed force will try to "take out" the communications of the enemy, first and foremost.

Whether it be by missile or cyber-attack, advanced armies seek to "blind the enemy," to prevent them from mounting a defence. Radar installations, satellites, key ministry buildings, radio and television signal broadcasters, power stations, airport runways, transport supply chains, and key defence-installations, are hit swiftly and first. Eliminating the means of communication of an enemy, can ensure swift success in combat. Remember this, when we examine wokeness.

Advanced communication is the key to success. Mastery of all forms of communication, can allow for better coordination of resources. Reach is improved. Audiences can be targeted. Marketing draws on these features. Today, marketing is optimised through the use of social media. Unfortunately, as we shall see, social media can also be weaponised, and used to advance arguments, subvert opinions, and ultimately deliver propaganda.

2.5 Control the seas

Another important lesson from World War Two, was the need to control the seas to have ultimate power. With control of the seas, a nation can control its production distribution, and also its flow of wealth, people, and indirectly, ideologies. Hitler knew this. His U-Boats (mini-submarines) had swung the early years of World War Two supremacy in his favour, as numerous allied naval and supply ships were sunk. They provided a valuable lesson for the wartime strategy employed today. Submarines are a "First-strike" weapon, that can deliver multiple warheads, by stealth. An effective means of defending a nation, through projecting strength away from geographic borders.

The loss of soldiers, armour and supplies, was hindering the ability of the allies to confront the enemy on foreign territories. Hitler knew he couldn't retain power and the control of Europe, without ruling the seas. Indeed, to venture beyond European shores, he had developed a massive naval fleet. This was headed by the feared "Bismarck" destroyer, which was dominating naval skirmishes in international waters.

This ship and its accompanying armada, were influential in the early years of the war. As such, the British and Americans were forced to rapidly expand the size, range and potency of their own naval fleets. Here, another power struggle ensued, which not only had a bearing on the outcome of World War Two, but also, on the current status quo of the world as we know it today.

The race was on. Control the seas and you have dominance. The greater your naval strength, the more you control the flow of strength, money, and wealth! Likewise, supremacy at sea, helped to protect the flow of oil from the Middle East oil-producing regions. Afterall, oil is the lifeblood of a thriving economy. Naval supremacy, also effectively, pushed a nations front line of defence away from its physical border. Any enemy would have to defeat you from afar.

The United States bore heavy losses on its Pacific naval fleet when it was attacked by the Japanese at Pearl Harbour in 1941. The pre-emptive early morning raid on the pride of the American fleet, as it was moored in Pearl Harbour (Hawaii), signalled the importance of control of the seas, as vital in winning a battle. The Japanese launched this audacious raid from their "six aircraft carrier fleet," a day before they officially declared war on the United States. Japan had unwittingly "awoken a giant" and drawn America into the war. The entry of the United States, had bought a super power into the conflict.

Naval supremacy which was attained by the United States (and to a lesser extent the British Navy), was later to end the war, and ultimately, change the world forever. German naval forces were eventually defeated, after allied plans to "sink the Bismarck," paid dividends. Soon after, Germany started losing control of its European territories. In the Asian Pacific region, the "Battle of Midway" had seen Japan have its naval forces suffer heavy losses, forcing it to retreat from its own goal, of invading and defeating Australia and surrounding countries. America could now amass significant armed forces throughout the South Pacific. A salient point, given the tension in the region today.

To win the war, Japan had to be defeated. America and its Allies, fought and regained control of the Philippines and the Marianas. These Island Colonies were under Japanese control. By taking them, the

Americans then had air bases closer to Japan and Tokyo, from which, they could launch bombing raids.

Direct bombing of Japanese fortifications on the mainland had now began, as American Air Force bombers were within reach, having taken off from the Marianas. However, Japan was still too far out of reach, to successfully amass a large invading ground force. America was unwilling to risk heavy casualties in trying to invade Japan.

At about the same time, scientists from around the world, were experimenting in nuclear fission. Albert Einstein had warned the American President Roosevelt that, it was important for America to gain an ascendancy in this field of warfare too, if it was to ultimately prevail.

Thereafter, the new incoming American President Harry Truman, had been informed that napalm fire-bombing of Japanese regions was proving successful. "Project Manhattan" had seen the development of the world's first atomic bomb. The greatest lesson of all time was about to be learnt. America didn't want to suffer the heavy losses that would have been incurred in a ground invasion of Japan.

In 1945, American air force bombers detonated two Atomic Bombs over the Japanese cities of Hiroshima and Nagasaki on August 6, and August 9, respectively. The destruction and enormity of what happened didn't sink in at first. Both cities were literally wiped off the map. Word of this annihilation was slow to reach Tokyo at first, such was the disbelief, at the power of these atomic bombs.

With large Russian forces also amassing at the Japanese border, the end was nigh for Japan. They formally surrendered shortly after (August 15,1945), on the deck of the "U.S.S. Missouri." With Germany being defeated in Europe, World War Two was over. The irony being, that this surrender was formalised on the deck of a naval destroyer that had given The United States "control of the seas." To this day, this control of the seas, has enabled The United States to retain its status as a leading super power and an economic juggernaut.

Russia too, had come through the ashes and rubble of the war, to emerge as a superpower, alongside America. These two nations then endured decades of a "Cold War." Here, there was fear and suspicion of each other, as the whole world feared their nuclear arsenal. Each, had a capability to destroy the world many times over.

2.6 Let sleeping dogs lie

The Allies had prevailed, but little did the world know, just what the repercussions would be, out of this worldwide mess. Like the first World War before it, society quickly regrouped, and set about taking advantage of the new found technologies derived from the advent of the war. Travel expanded and trade exploded, as the seas became a highway for cargo transmission.

The dollars flowed, wealth creation was the order of the day, and the war was soon long forgotten, though suspicion remained about the actions and motives of old enemies. Taking advantage of this too, were the geographically large, and well populated, countries of Russia and China.

The end of the war, had left their respective communist regimes largely intact and their dictators unopposed. These countries went about their way, quietly amassing wealth without the heavy, obvious trade advantages of their Western counterparts. The rising GDP levels, and booming economies of the developed Western nations, had relegated these communist countries to a minor after-thought. The "Cold War" between the United Soviet Socialist Republic and the United States seemingly came and went. The fear of a nuclear exchange, so graphically demonstrated at Hiroshima and Nagasaki, had in the end, seen "common sense" and "cool heads" prevail.

Nuclear disarmament treaties were signed, and the world breathed a collective sigh of relief, as the two protagonists set about arms reduction (though not to a level low enough to undermine their strategic strength).

Unfortunately, at the same time, "nuclear proliferation" saw a number of other countries join the arms race. France, Germany, The United Kingdom, Israel, India, Pakistan, China, Japan, and the two Koreas, had joined the main two combatants in becoming nuclear-armed. All of a sudden, the world as we know it, could be destroyed at the mere push of a button, by many nations. One hell of a deterrent for any nation or force considering instigating a war in the quest for power.

Has this over-riding fear of annihilation through nuclear warfare, so pervaded our mindset, that it is foremost in influencing our behaviour? That is to say, is this fear now so entrenched in our makeup, that we can push boundaries and antagonise, and yet know deep down, that a worst-case scenario will never be reached?

A whole new generation of humanity has never lived through the "horror of war." Have the exploits of two great wars, created a complacency among those of the West, about their safety? Freedom from prior sacrifices appears to be taken for granted. Safe from foreign enemies, a lot of Western nations are now having to confront an enemy from within. One that was borne out of their own economic success!

People and nations are willing to push their argument, without the fear of a finite retribution, knowing that no one wants that outcome. Collectively at a national level, this worst-case scenario is hopefully, unlikely to be reached.

However, as individuals, have we all been conditioned to know that consequences for our actions are trivial, compared to those facing mankind in general? Analysis of this human behaviour is important when understanding the arguments for or against relevant political persuasions. Why, frustratingly, is there now an emerging "culture war" that is becoming more heated, with no end in sight?

2.7 The increasing power of scientists

Before we analyse this, there is one final lesson to be learnt from the previous deeds of the great wars. The end of the second World War, was expedited by the frightening exploits of the scientists at work for the combatant nations. "Nuclear fission" was only the start of things. While it created an end game, it opened up a can of worms strategically. Nations sought ways of increasing their military strength, whilst at the same time, minimising their economic costs and casualty levels.

The advent of long-range missiles with great destructive force, also gave rise to the more secretive experimenting in chemical and biological warfare. This was already being covertly explored, pending the success of the atomic bomb, during World War Two. The ability to be able to deliver a warhead tipped with a chemical or biological agent, was mischievously being sought.

Delivered to a city with a large population, biological and chemical agents could quickly render the inhabitants, either incapacitated or worse still, deceased. All without risking "life and limb" by putting combat soldiers in harm's way. The financial cost of this warfare was, relatively speaking, very minimal.

Thankfully, the horrific trauma these "weapons of mass destruction" may impose, quickly saw them condemned and banned by the United Nations. The world was unanimous in the need for their eradication, and any use of them, has since been mandated as a serious war crime against humanity. Alas, this has not stopped their production, the stock-piling of them, nor the experimenting with them to make them more potent and lethal. Scary too, is the fact that terrorists would love to get hold of them and would have no hesitation in using them.

If anything, these weapons have further enhanced the "levels of suspicion" countries have of one another. Secrecy about their existence, coupled with espionage, surveillance, and cyber-crime (hacking or attacking computer hardware), have all taken the world to a more dangerous and unsafe level of overall safety and wellbeing.

This has further emphasized the need and urgency for a greater understanding of the real battle that is at stake today. Technology has complicated the competing economic virtues of capitalism versus the social complexities of communism. These two competing political ideologies have been "vying for centre stage" for centuries. Only now that the world has become a global village, has the battle become more intense, as recent events have shown. Due to the irreversible damage a global nuclear conflict may inflict, a "New Cold War" is emerging as a threat.

This time between the main protagonists, The United States and communist China. At its heart, are the opposing views of socialism versus capitalism. So much so, that other nations are finding themselves drawn to one political persuasion or the other. Two distinct sides are being formed. Simultaneously, this war has morphed into smaller factional contests between individuals and relatively small groups within each nation. It has spawned the culture wars of today, which are being contested amongst the populations of various Western nations. Further, these battles have quickly been politicised by political parties, television broadcasters, and through the manipulation of the internet.

The scientists themselves, have been weaponised, as they are summonsed to support or refute various issues. It seems that they are no longer immune to corruption, just like the rest of society. There appear to be no shortage of scientific experts willing to say that global warming is rampant and very real. Why then, are there just as many scientists refuting their claims? Why is the media only telling one side of the story?

3

When Simplicity Gives Way to Complexity

3.1 Learning

Look closely at the title of this book. Seven simple words. It doesn't get any easier in theory, yet the greatest dilemma facing society, can be encapsulated in seven measly words. There is a beauty and simplicity in their literal meaning. Let's take them one at a time.

"Learning" is a foundation bedrock upon which, all proud nations are built, although it often taken for granted. Increasing knowledge through education and learned experiences, expands opportunities. It is at the forefront of scientific research. It can lead to greater technology, higher levels of productivity, and advances in medicine, to name but a few. All of which combine to raise overall living standards.

A simple, noble pursuit that helps our youth mature into upstanding citizens in their mature, adult life. It is no surprise, that the most prosperous nations with high economic growth, also have the highest education standards in the world. It is a key performance indicator for economic growth. Governments today, spend a large proportion of their budgetary revenue on providing infrastructure to ensure its future populace is highly educated. This ensures longevity for a nation and a better quality of life for the individual.

This has a multiplier effect of ensuring that civil obedience is maintained, as the inhabitants of the land obey the law, and behave in an orderly fashion to keep public order. Likewise, with a higher education, there should be less reliance on social welfare. The unemployed, physically and mentally impaired, and the elderly, can be a drain on public finances. Government debt levels have to be monitored closely, to prevent the dreaded recession or depression, caused by diminishing economic growth. "In a nutshell," learning is vital.

3.2 Right

"Right" is one of those words of the English dictionary which can have three vastly different meanings, despite the same spelling. It can be as simple as having the correct answer or opinion, or even the best way of doing things. We all wish to accomplish tasks, pass exams, and avoid breaking the law, so we quickly learn what "right" is all about.

"Right" can also refer to an individual's independence, and his or her justification in carrying out their activity in a manner they deem fit. It creates a sense of entitlement and individualism, as people can say what they wish, and believe what they want. All harmless, provided the law is obeyed, nobody gets hurt, and no disharmony is created. In this instance, the opposite occurs, which is then "wrong." More on this later.

One interesting point on "right." To have rights, requires liberty and freedom of expression. This can only be derived from a political system that encourages this. Capitalism springs to mind. One of its most redeeming features, is that it permits the right to free speech. Try saying what you wish in a communist state, and see how long you live or remain free. "Right" is not a cheap word and should not be taken for granted.

Others still, conversely, will initially perceive the word "right" as a direction. These people will often see the word "right" and find the word "left" quickly wanting to "roll off the tongue." No problem with that, as "right" like it's "left" counterpart, is an integral part of a life skill known as navigating. If you are not perfectly balanced or going perfectly straight ahead, you are either going left or right. (that applies to falling too!). This is all simple isn't it? We all know the basic meaning of "right" one way or another.

3.3 From

Life is fast-paced. You have to grab opportunities when they present themselves, to make the most out of life. From the minute you are born, you are growing. As an individual, an ideal maybe, a small company or even a country, change and growth are inevitable. How fast this occurs, is dependent on many social, physical, biological, and economic factors. Regardless of which, the key thing to remember about the word "from," is that it implies deviation from an original point.

A difference is created out of change. This can be in the form of distance, size, time, opinion, or anything else that is quantifiable. This is also a necessity when it comes to evolution. Charles Darwin's "survival of the fittest" theory, clearly demonstrated that positive changes are quickly adapted, are inherited, and ultimately aid in the survival of a species.

Change can be good. A "point of difference" is vital when it comes to marketing and profitability. It can create wealth, improve enjoyment, lead to the eradication of diseases, improve education, and can help develop better relationships. Whist change can unfortunately, often have negative consequences, the human brain is fortuitously "wired" to protect us from harm, danger, pain, and unpleasant experiences. We are "wired" to understand, differentiate, and distinguish between various entities and what is good or bad for us.

It should be noted here, that "from" also has a historical context. For something to have changed, some period of time needs to have elapsed. Simple basic physics here, but history brings with it experience.

Now this can be good or bad, but either way, it helps to shape future behaviour.

They say "a rolling stone shall gather no moss." By moving from one place to another you can perhaps, experience different things, or even gain momentum if you are on a bicycle rolling down a hill! On the other hand, if things remain idle, cobwebs accrue, metals rust, food goes stale, the "rot sets in," and change becomes more difficult. In essence, great things can come from change and difference. But these have to be learnt first, often the hard way. They say "if you haven't ever made a mistake, you are not really trying." "From" is in essence, proof of learning or change, which are both derived from history.

3.4 Wong

You will not find the word "wong" in the English dictionary. Unless you are dyslexic that is. But there is no hidden agenda here. This word has no meaning and does not exist. Pick up the American comic "Marvel" and you may find reference to the fictitious character "Wong." On the other hand, if you are searching for a phone number, you are sure to come across "Wong" in a Chinese phone directory. There are many of Chinese descent that are likely to have "Wong" as their Christian or surnames. The point of "wong" in this book title, is to make reference to an error or mistake. To know what is truly right, also requires us to know the consequence of being wrong. (Or truly left!)

We are all guilty of making mistakes every day. We even tell lies to cover them up. But sooner or later, these mistakes come back to haunt us. They "bite us on the bum" and we do not make the same mistake twice. That is, if we do not learn from history, we will not progress as individuals, entities or nations. And sooner or later, we pay the price.

Has anyone detected the irony in the miss-spelling of the word "wrong" as "wong?" There are two points to make here. Firstly, it serves to highlight our falling education standards. Australia is currently slipping in overall educational levels, according to world comparison charts. Our literacy and numeracy rankings are falling below countries of much lower socio-economic status. Does anyone in Government care and what is being done to arrest this slide? This does not bode well, for our continuing ability to compete on the world stage, nor to adequately cater for the demands of our population in the coming years.

Second point. The spelling and pronunciation of "wong" is synonymous with the encroaching of all things China. It seems that the rise of China is going to be a major problem for our nation and indeed, the world at large. China seems to be implicated in a lot of local and international tensions today. Their influence is everywhere. Including in "the title of this book."

Whether it be, a burgeoning population, a dangerous communist government, denial of spreading diseases such as covid-19 around the world, invading neighbouring countries, taking control of the South Pacific Seas, spying, cyber-attacks, infiltrating foreign political systems, or even spelling mistakes, China is in our face. Why are there not more people willing to speak up and confront this issue? And for those who do try to speak out, why are they not being listened to? Who is trying to silence these people who speak up? Why do they or should they, feel intimidated?

3.5 Wrong

The position one find's themselves in, if they have done something incorrectly. Do this many times in an exam and you are sure to fail! If you get on the incorrect side of the road while in a vehicle, it can have serious or deadly consequences. "Wrong" is the extreme opposite of "right." It refers to an error being made, which will need to be corrected for learning to occur. To be "in the wrong," is to be guilty of an offense or to take the incorrect stance on an issue.

The dictionary also considers "wrong" to be unlawful, lawless, illegal, and immoral. Even dishonest. Consider these salient points, when you hear the arguments coming from the left, in today's political sphere. What is it with the lefties in their denial of the truth, their willingness to disobey the law, and their defying of conventional wisdom?

As an evolving species, we have learnt quickly, the difference between "right and wrong," and it's the primary reason why we are all here today. Just like how pain inflicted from an injury is a defensive mechanism, we are programmed to learn, especially from our mistakes.

Indeed, scientists say the average human brain only uses up about two percent of its potential. Clearly, there is much more to be learnt. But are we getting smarter? We need to continually improve education standards, in order to minimize errors that are made, but this is clearly not happening. Our literacy and numeracy levels are in a frightening decline. Pretty sad for a First World nation enjoying the prosperity that we do.

Is the world becoming a better and safer place? Do we all, always have the best intentions at heart, and are we all thinking clearly with similar objectives? What the hell has hampered our progress and slowed overall economic growth? Why are poverty levels rising and living standards dropping? Why is social unrest on the rise throughout the world? Why is democracy under threat, with liberty and freedom of speech being curtailed?

3.6 Woke

Think closely about the title of this book, and how it is going through a "transition and re-correction" as you decipher it. "Woke" appears in the title and it sits between "right and left." You could even say that there is also something "wrong" about this, as it is closest to the word "left." It is a trendy word that is on everyone's lips these days, but what the hell does it mean or represent?

Put simply, "woke" merely refers to a raised awareness about inequality. Seemingly any inequality. But boy, hasn't it had a profound effect on just about everything in society. Despite our obsession with perpetual economic growth, there has always been a compassionate understanding and awareness of those less fortunate. After all, the first priority of government, is the health and safety of its whole population.

Governments have used social policy to share the wealth created through welfare payments, public education, public housing, and healthcare for all. This is to avoid alienating any minority group, and to appear impartial and unbiased about all relevant issues. However, as economic growth occurs, there is always a delay in the redistribution of this new found wealth. This comes through the taxation system.

This has led to a growing resentment towards the "elite ruling classes" of society. Natural forces of human behaviour, have also seen the economically disadvantaged (poor people) tend to reside together in slums, enclaves, or in regions where real estate is relatively affordable. Again, this is furthering division between the poor and affluent within communities. To help deal with this inequality and encourage inclusivity, high profile members of society have strived to act and speak in a politically-correct manner.

Wokeness has spawned; where greater emphasis is now being placed on equality in terms of social, rather than purely economic factors. It has consumed us. The feel-good factor of a "few nice consoling words," it seems, is clearly more deliverable than a "few bucks."

The "woke" brigade are somewhat, deranged. They cannot even use pronouns such as "he" or "she," as they have to opted for binary gender terminology. In other words, they believe using "he" or "she" may cause offense to the opposite sex, or those who are bisexual, or those who are transgender. Spare me please!

The advent of advanced forms of communication, mass media coverage at saturation levels, Orwellian-like surveillance (think George Orwell in his futuristic novel "1984"), and the world wide web, have each placed us all under increased scrutiny. This is strangling our freedom of speech and our liberty. Even the words we use, are under scrutiny. The invasion of wokeness is an attack on our language. Another step towards totalitarian behaviour.

Coupled with the growing disparity between the "haves" and "have nots," there is a rising social revolution whereby, those not being seen as politically correct, are being called out and vilified by disgruntled individuals and minority groups. This is considered "woke" behaviour, where devotees now deride any individual, ideology, belief or agenda, which does not fit "their narrative."

It has spawned the "culture wars" and "cancel culture" that are permeating our society today. Interestingly, the woke brigade are most vocal in the successful Western nations, where democracy has been fought for and maintained. You could almost say that "wokeness" is a tool used to weaken the wealthy, and to give power to the less fortunate. It certainly, is not fiscally responsible to appease "non contributors" and "keyboard warriors." Nor should these faceless individuals who send derogatory and malicious emails, and who post biased, offensive material on social platforms be "kowtowed" to. Policies that can be morally beneficial to society, usually come at a high cost. Renewable energy is a prime example.

These culture wars are numerous, and are impacting our everyday quality of life. They are affecting decision making by planners and governments. People are having to adjust their behaviour and express themselves carefully, so as not to offend anyone who may appear disadvantaged to the "woke" brigade. "Equality for all" is their mantra, as the woke brigade seek their "utopia." An imaginary, perfect place, where everyone is the same in terms of equal wealth, health and social status, and where the perfect political system regulates all of this.

Conversely though, they say "to go woke, is to go broke." This is also creating a resentment and tension among the rest of the population. Some of us can see the fallacy of this, but common sense is being swept away, by a propaganda machine "spruiking" the merits of socialist policy.

Since the dawn of time, man and the nations that have evolved, have always had differing opinions on economic, social, religious, cultural, and political matters. For the most part, we have all got along amicably, despite the differences of opinion. Wokeness has reared its ugly head, with those feeling disparaged or disadvantaged, no longer willing to abide with the general consensus or systems in place. It has created a conflict among the populace, within the borders of respective countries. Wokeness is a problem that needs to be resolved quickly, because it is now causing social unrest and political upheaval. So much so, that illegal activity is starting to go unpunished.

The recent protests against the death of George Floyd in America, saw peaceful protests hijacked by the "left" socialist minorities. We all saw the riots, the looting, and the lawlessness that ensued. Of note, was that the violence was at its worst in cities governed by local mayors who were progressives (left-leaning). These elected officials chose not to enforce law and order during the protests. The result was anarchy, death, and billions of dollars in damage to local cities. This has only created more unrest, and further heightened social tensions.

And most concerningly of all, while many nations have been distracted by internal feuding and bickering, other nations such as China, have been quietly amassing economic wealth and military might. Indeed, this nation is even forcefully and stealthily acquiring land from neighbouring countries, and fortifying it, as a means of preserving its own strategic strength. It is time that nations "refocus" on the important matters that are really relevant, rather than pursuing idealistic policies that are being put forward by the "woke" brigade.

3.7 Left

The four letters of the word "left," when looked at fleetingly, instantly bring thoughts of direction. This is pretty important knowledge to have, driving on the busy roads of Australia, the United Kingdom, and other like-minded nations. Inherent knowledge of "left," while driving automobiles, keeps us safe from head-on collisions.

Numerically, a greater proportion of the population also know in the back of their mind, that "left" also implies weakness. Given most of us are right-handed and right-footed, we are clumsy and uncoordinated when it comes to using our left limbs. Again, no problem here, as our brains have told us that we are more efficient and coordinated using our right limbs.

Conversely, left-handed people, have the same deficiencies and limitations in their corresponding right limbs. Again, no problem here, and I will leave it to the geneticists, biologists, and maybe the historians, to work out why the disproportionate level of right-handed members of society. The overall point to remember though, is that we all have a bias to the left or right, for reasons unknown, and this appears genetically "wired" into us.

"Left" also indirectly implies that time has elapsed, and that someone or something is no longer there. In other words, it refers to a new absence, as what or who you were looking for, has left, has departed, or is not there anymore.

Another connotation of "left," is that it can also refer to that portion which remains or is a surplus. Rather ironic, that surplus should be synonymous with "left," as we shall see in coming chapters. Over all though, "left" appears to be a harmless little word and seemingly, just plays a "balancing-act" type of role with its antonym "right" in our language and psyche.

4

The Political Combatants

4.1 Throwing fuel on the fire

Seven harmless little words as the title of a book sitting quietly on a bookshelf. Put on your political glasses and they become the words of our time. They represent the enormous upheaval that has recently taken place in our society. One that has been rapid, and which has taken the world to the very edge. It seems that every action and reaction, is now viewed from a political perspective. What we see and what we are being told, is now weaponised as well. What ever happened to objectivity? What chance do our children and future generations have, if they are being brain-washed with subjective views of events and current affairs? What ever happened to telling and reporting the truth?

Growing up, we all quickly learnt "right from wrong." It was a sharp learning curve accelerated by negative experiences when we got things wrong. Our parents were the first to tell us if we exhibited the wrong behaviour, by disciplining us. Mum and dad also quickly taught us to count to ten, sing the alphabet, and learn right from left. These skills served us well, right up until high school, where our education begins to accelerate rapidly. Our parents, then relied on our teachers to educate us to a higher level. With this, comes the ability to rationalise and reason, which is vital for an individual and for society in general, to continue to grow and prosper.

Throw politics into the education curriculum however, and all hell breaks loose. A vast majority of secondary school children and teenagers in general, are today, disinterested in politics as it's uncool, boring, irrelevant, and definitely "not on their radar." As this cohort contemplate leaving school or university to enter the work force, a large proportion of them have little or no interest in politics, as they are seduced by money and the need to accumulate wealth. Of course, an interest in the opposite sex also takes precedence at about this age too! For most that is! I don't want to be seen as homophobic!

The only time politics is given consideration, is when our new crop of school leavers have to vote at local, state or federal elections. Even then, a vast majority often cannot be bothered getting on the electoral roll, or will only vote to avoid a penalty or infringement notice. Many, certainly, give little thought to who they vote for. Many individuals vote for who their parents or friends vote for. Some others do a "donkey vote" to reflect their dismay at the political system in general. Others still, recklessly vote for minority parties with silly names, such as "the Marijuana party." In other words, they are often throwing their vote away, with little regard to its pending relevance.

Political persuasion (your preferred allegiance to a particular style of political governance), is a subjective choice for all individuals. And it should remain so! Differences of opinion or ideas can lead to new initiatives, a greater uptake of new technology, and the embracing of new ideas. These can further socio-economic development, through reforms and changes which allow democracy to thrive, and which drive prosperity. Or so we thought.

"A change is as good as a break." Over the years, Australia and other nations, have alternately been governed by left or right-leaning political parties and for the most part, enjoyed relative prosperity with both forms of government. As such, very few parents have had the time, the foresight, or the patience to explain to their children, the significant differences between the political parties.

So many parents themselves, do not pay too much attention to where their vote goes, or where their political allegiances lie, or why so. Others, including migrants who become nationalised and eligible to vote, or those who speak little English, often have no idea who they are voting for, or even abstain from voting at all. The pool, from which votes for electable government are drawn, is now "murky."

Political aspirants at all levels of government, are now concerning themselves more with getting elected, than they are with being capable of governing equally and effectively. This is a shame in a time of such inequality, disparity, and general rising global tensions that we are seeing now.

There is also a growing problem regarding what these future voters are being taught at school about differing political systems. It is obvious, that what was once the delivery of an objective education, has morphed into a politically-biased propaganda curriculum. It is little wonder that our education standards are slipping. While "Maths and English" continue to remain as core subjects, the arts, literature, and history subjects, are no longer appearing popular or relevant as elective subjects. They are being quickly neglected and forgotten. The curriculum is now catering more for career-specific subjects in information technology and design, or studies in social humanities.

With a wider array of subjects on offer, teachers have never been busier, and resources never as scarce. You "ignore history at your own peril!" Close study of ancient and modern history, reveals many rulers, empires, and societies that have arisen, conquered, and failed for varying reasons throughout the ages. But this point no longer seems pertinent.

Although it must be said, our rapidly changing society, and its rising living costs, are necessitating the study of subjects that lead to "fruitful" employment. Gone are the days of doing what you enjoy. There is a growing tendency to studying for careers that create the best prospects for employment. The "need for money" is becoming "ingrained."

Conquests and significant developments of yesteryear, have been quickly forgotten, and consigned to the history books. The main point to note here, is that no civilisation or country has been able to conquer and rule the whole planet. To not learn from this, is a failure of us as individuals, but also as a species. This requires the objective, diligent teaching of history and the social sciences by the teaching fraternity.

It also requires a willing student body, eager to embrace a knowledge of the past. Afterall, our students of today, are the workers and leaders of tomorrow. Should the decline in teaching of history and social sciences continue, there will be a growing number of uninformed, impressionable young or novice voters in the future.

It is also important, that education is delivered in an objective manner. Young adults are quite often easily influenced through peer group pressure. Likewise, their ability to reason and rationalise is not fully developed, even though they are mostly aware of what is right and wrong. They are often "spoon-fed" a subjective view or opinion on curriculum topics, which can later corrupt their future personal beliefs and behaviour. Most concerning, is that many do not even realise this, and no one seems capable of addressing this.

There will be a significant disparity in the political persuasion of young voters, into the future, because of this. It is almost as if there is an agenda being met. The coercion of young minds, is now rampant in our secondary and tertiary institutions. Afterall, it was Vladimir Lenin, the renowned communist who touted, "give me four years to teach the children and the seed I have sown, will never be uprooted."

Stagnating economic growth, rising inequality, and social unrest between the "haves" and "have nots," have only served to strengthen the differences between differing political persuasions, and the resultant methods of governing.

As economic growth is slowing worldwide, countries have relied on population growth to sustain demand, and avoid the dreaded recessions (two consecutive quarters of negative GDP growth), or worse still, a depression. Governments in countries such as Australia, even resort to offering baby bonuses and generous child support welfare to families, just to encourage natural population growth and replenishment.

Again, we see this obsession with economic growth at play. They say "there is safety in numbers." Economists say this comes from a thriving, expanding, wealthy populace. The strength and power of a nation, is ultimately, a measure of the size and wealth of a nation's population.

To further emphasize this, immigration is used to bolster the growth. It is seen internationally, as cooperative and "socially noble," to undertake a generous immigration program, and thereby share the wealth of the nation. Nowhere more so than in Australia, which is blessed with abundant natural resources, and which enjoys an enviable climate. But politicians, now more importantly, view immigrants as a means of boosting economic numbers, thereby enhancing their credentials as competent, responsible economic managers. Afterall, "once in power, nobody has a desire to relinquish their position of strength."

This in turn, makes governing parties highly re-electable, as the living standards and wealth of the populace rise. But this is now fraught with its own dangerous repercussions, and will pose its own problems in years to come. Mass immigration, combined with industrialisation, is seeing a massive number of workers displaced from their employment. Job opportunities are disappearing, and there is a reluctance by many, to "roll up the sleeves" and get dirty. There is a resistance to moving away from the over-crowded cities to rural regions to work on the land. Likewise, expensive service provision is now more fiscally-responsible when it is delivered in a centralised manner.

Coupled with crippling rises in the costs of living, there are many jobs going unfilled, as they do not generate a wage high enough to sustain a decent standard of living. Housing affordability has diminished so much, that many have given up on the Australian dream of "owning your own home." This has created a large cohort of disaffected young Australians, angry at not being able to get ahead.

They feel that capitalism has failed them. Are the disillusioned young, driving the uprising in socialism? Worse still, in years to come, nobody will be able to maintain a decent standard of living, if they work in the food provision and service sectors. How will this planet, with its burgeoning population, continue to feed itself?

It seems that the Third World dwellers (those used to subsistence means of living), are the only people prepared to work for a miserly wage. Immigrants from countries of lower socio-economic status, are the only individuals willing to take the low-paid job opportunities. This is growing the divide between the expectation and the reality of a capitalist system. It is widening the gap between the well-to-do, and the not-so-fortunate. Social unrest is on the increase.

This is most evident in countries such as Australia, with its relatively small, incumbent population. The wealth, nationality, religion, culture, belief, and noticeably, political persuasion of these immigrants, is having a massive impact on the composition and wellbeing of the host nations. Despite being very multicultural, natural forces of human behaviour have given rise to settlement into tribes. A shared language and religious or cultural beliefs, are seeing the formation of enclaves. Will big government fail and see the reformation of colonies once more?

Election results at a local, state and federal level, have and will continue to be, skewed by heavy immigration. A new political allegiance may be formed or reinforced by the existing personal political prejudices of those migrating. Local governing politicians can often be elected, according to their ethnicity or nationality, when their electorate is dominated by one major ethnic group, such as the Chinese for instance. Many devious political figures now engage in "branch stacking," where new political members enter the political domain, having the backing of a particular ethnic cohort of voters. This can falsely boost the popularity of an individual, making them highly electable among their peers.

Political parties are now more susceptible to losing elections and the right to govern, through demographic and social forces, rather than through their record of economic management and performance. As such, it is even more imperative to understand the fundamental differences between left and right, when it comes to political persuasion.

Our future security, stability, safety, and economic wellbeing, have and always will, be dependent on it.

4.2 The modern dilemma

It was often thought, and readily acknowledged, that to win power and govern, a political party had to have social and economic policy that pleased the sensible centre. This is where the general population (most voters) sits, in terms of overall opinion. Most people don't have time for politics, and they only pay fleeting attention to it, when it is time to vote.

So, the smart politicians are always chasing the popular vote. This is best done by addressing policy issues that would please the greatest proportion of the population. The major parties, traditionally, seek to deliver on policies which can be implemented with relative ease, and at a minimal cost to the taxpayer. Common sense and wise to do.

However, times have changed. Greater media exposure, wokeness, and greater economic disparity, have all given voice to the more extreme, passionate, hard-left and hard-right supporters of political parties. To be seen to be of the extreme left or right, was previously considered as being too radical and polarising. Controversial even. It was certainly stigmatising, and generally not recommended or respected, if you wanted to remain popular and socially accepted. And definitely, not a platform upon which, to build a political party.

Alas, the politically correct environment in which we exist, has seen politics diluted by numerous culture wars. These have detracted from the traditional policy issues, over which, parties fought in order to gain power (to govern). These culture wars have given greater power and voice to the radical extremists of the left, in particular. Therein, lies the greatest threat to society as we know it.

So, who and what are the two mainstream parties, that are the combatants, fighting for power and control in most developed nations? They represent the belief systems of those on the right and those of the left. Simple really, but made complicated by the fact that the left has been monstered by virtue signalling entities, who have highjacked their respective ideologies.

Regardless of which Western nation you relate this discussion to, the arguments of both sides are the same. The simplest way to briefly summarize, and understand the main features of these two ideologies, is to look at the battles for government within the "five eyes" nations.

Out of World War Two, an espionage alliance was formed between The United Kingdom, The United States of America, Canada, Australia, and New Zealand. This was designed to share, covertly, any intelligence pertaining to the communication systems, so inherent in the wellbeing of these five countries. These five prominent First World nations all have a few things in common.

Through capitalism, they have all experienced vast economic growth, and enjoy some of the highest living standards in the world. These same five countries, to this very day, share intelligence, remain firm allies, enjoy significant trade amongst themselves, and are the envy of the free world, in terms of their sovereignty, freedom and democracy.

Predominantly English-speaking nations, they also all share similar cultural and religious beliefs. A strong faith in the Catholic and Christian church has helped in maintaining law and order in these nations. They are respectable, peace-abiding nations eager to grow, prosper and thrive, virtue of the democracy created by their stable parliamentary systems.

Yet, it is as if they have become victims of their own success. Nowhere is the battle between left and right more pronounced, than within these countries. It is here, that the differences between the left and right have become so blatantly obvious. As we move through the 21st century, these differences have become such a highly contentious issue for these respective nations to deal with.

4.3 The right capitalists

The ongoing strength of these nations, has undoubtedly been attained through growth, achieved by predominantly right-leaning governments, which have embraced capitalism and all its virtues. Sensible, conservative folk have worked hard to secure a healthy and often wealthy, means of existence for themselves. Entrepreneurialism has been encouraged and allowed to thrive, as a means to create wealth.

Coupled with rapid industrialization, wealth grew quickly and Gross Domestic Product (GDP) levels rose ahead of other nations. Incentives to achieve business success are provided through progressive taxation systems, where the burden of paying tax falls proportionally on the higher earning individuals, and on the more profitable companies. Individuals and companies are able to prosper through taxation systems that are fair, and not too exorbitant, and without excessive rules and regulations, which can stifle and discourage growth.

Out of this profit-inducing growth, successive right-leaning governments have been able to moderately tax the wealth creators, and redistribute the profits in the form of welfare payments to the less fortunate members of society. These nations are able to run their economies in a balanced, conservative manner, as tax revenue gained is dispersed among the populace. Conservative spending by right-leaning political parties, also ensures that public debt is minimized, so as to prevent a debt burden that will have to be paid back by future generations. It has also provided a revenue source that has been instrumental in ensuring the safety and security of these nations, through greater spending on defence, and on law and order.

The imposition of comparatively moderate taxes still gave an incentive for inhabitants to work, invest, and grow their wealth. Living standards and life-expectancy have grown to levels that are the envy of the rest of the world under capitalism.

The conservative right-leaning governments have, traditionally, always been wise managers of federal budgets. They pride themselves in being the best economic managers, and strive to have an overall budget surplus. That is, greater taxation revenue which exceeds the cost of total government spending.

Strict management of this revenue has also traditionally, aided in financing, the continued advances in health and education standards enjoyed by all Australians. Strong competition between the public and private sectors in both health and education, has seen Australia achieve an enviable level of service provision, and further development in both portfolios.

But these sectors are also coming under greater scrutiny and pressure, as the population increases and our cost of living increases dramatically. The ongoing funding of both sectors, is a delicate balancing-act. As more people require financial assistance just to live and "make ends meet," the government budget can only stretch so far. As such, the wealthy have a tendency to opt for private health care and private education. While more expensive, and generally considered superior in terms of quality, this does create a division in society.

The less fortunate rely on public education, where there is growing debate about how Australia can arrest its declining education levels. It seems that public education is not keeping up to previous high standards. And there is an agenda at play, within the education system. It appears that there is a growing discontent, at the curriculum and how it is being delivered. Is this curriculum being delivered in an objective and unbiased manner? Apparently not.

Regardless of this, our higher education standards at the tertiary level, are very attractive to overseas students. Expensive university degrees, are eagerly sought and paid for by overseas Chinese students, which is helping the "bottom line" for our University Chancellors. The government also encourages this, because it also fuels economic growth by creating more demand for housing, accommodation, goods, and services.

A strong belief in law and order is also significant among the right-leaning conservatives. The growth of wealth is pointless if it cannot be preserved and protected. Civil order, and abiding by the laws of the land, are a key feature of successful capitalist nations. It creates a sense of freedom and liberty. Freedom of speech allows all voices to be heard in a peaceful manner, as well as allowing the right to free protest if desired.

With continuing economic success, there has always for the main part, been a large proportion of the populace (conservatives) that want society to progress along these same lines. These people will traditionally always vote for parties of the right. Unfortunately, there are always those that don't share the same views, participate in the work force, or share evenly, in the wealth created. Their perception being, that there is a better way to "grow the pie" and share it more evenly.

4.4 The Socialist left

People who vote for political parties of the left persuasion, are generally socialists, and are also known as the progressives. They are big on spending, and believe that ownership, control and distribution of wealth, capital, land, and resources, should be by the community as a whole. Their progressive ideology, calls for free health and education, greater public housing provision, and any other means to reduce inequality between the "haves" and the "have nots."

This is all well and good, but someone has got to pay for it. Unfortunately, those of the left, have traditionally overspent and increased the debt levels of their societies. They are more concerned with wealth distribution than they are wealth creation. As mentioned before, "left" can refer to a surplus. Ironically though, left-leaning governments have big budget deficits, with no surplus to be found anywhere.

The lefties then have to impose greater taxes on the working population, in order to generate enough revenue to finance this extravagant expenditure. Higher taxes create a disincentive to work and as a result, have an overall effect of driving down productivity. The revenue burden then falls, predominantly, on the diminishing private sector to drive future growth.

Those self-employed, entrepreneurial types wishing to work harder (as profits are their own), then end up getting taxed even more. The paradox being, that the greater their success, the more the leftists want them taxed. This slowly manifests itself in a silent at first, but then a louder, growing resentment towards the high-income earners. The entrepreneurs of the right, seek to avoid paying tax as best they can, while the leftists, seek new ways to impose taxes to extract revenue to fund their socialist ideologies. This itself, splits the left and right on the issue of the best method of growing the economic pie.

Gradually, as socialism spreads, government debt levels soar. Expenditure vastly outpaces a receding revenue stream, as the private sector diminishes. History has shown that overtime, as economic hardship takes hold, leftist governments then often have to print cash, just to keep their economy afloat. The true value of a dollar diminishes, as it is no longer "worked for."

Falling productivity then gives way to rapid inflation, which sends the cost of living soaring. Eventually, poverty rises dramatically, social unrest increases, the economy collapses, and what little money that is left, is corruptly retained by the government. This in turn, fuels aggression amongst the general population, and creates the perfect environment for social revolutions.

Socialist policies are fantastic in theory. Everyone wants a harmonious world where there is no war, where living standards grow, and where there is no inequality. Stable governments, evenly providing wealth, health, and education is the goal of all nations. A competing goal too however, is to ensure these principles are maintained into the future. As such, defence and security are necessary to facilitate future growth. Inherent in this, is law and order. This is a key staple in a modern wealthy society and until recently, it has been taken for granted.

A Society governed in an orderly manner, is able to preserve and protect people and property.

The leftist ideology, also places a slightly greater value on social issues such as race, nationality, culture, ethnicity, religion, and even sexual persuasion. This is to appeal to a greater audience who may otherwise, opt for the safer, conservative "right" way of voting along economic considerations.

So, we have two contrasting preferred political persuasions. The "right," based on capitalism and all its virtues, has stood the test of time historically. We are living testimony to its success. However, some while sharing in this success, are also ideologically driven to evenly redistribute this through left-leaning beliefs. Society is a victim of its own success in creating wealth. This wealth, needs to be redistributed thoughtfully, conservatively, and most importantly, transparently.

If this doesn't occur, rampant spending and the adaption of socialist policy, can ultimately see a transition away from capitalism. Subtle at first, it can evolve into a state of communism, where wealth and ideas become part of a collective whole. And communism needs to be avoided. History has shown, that communism was fought and defeated in two World Wars. It has bought misery, poverty, ethnic cleansing, and overall declining individual prosperity, to communist countries.

Worse still, though, is that liberty and freedom of speech are eroded by the ruling communist parties. To maintain control of a repressed population, communist parties attempt to control all assets, education, and thoughts, as well as strictly monitor, all forms of media and communication. They seek to silence dissent, and those within the population, who question this form of government.

As the voice of leftist socialists has grown, they have become obsessed with attaining power through any means possible. Supporters of the left have, over the years, generally been subtle in their parochialism for socialism, but in recent times, this has been replaced by a deluded, blatant disregard of capitalism. This has become an ever-complicated issue in the globalised free world of today.

4.5 The greens and independents

Aside from the mainstream left and right parties, each Western nation, also has a few small Independent parties, which can never attract enough votes to win the seats required to form government in their own right.

In predominantly Western nations, politics is also currently being plagued by the "nuisance value" of the Green parties. The Greens are traditionally, a party that concerned themselves with defending the natural environment. Emanating from the 1960's and 1970's, the feel-good hippy movement, helped give rise to a generation of young people who fought for the preservation of the environment.

This usually involved opposing any government policies which were likely to have an adverse effect on the planet. "Greenpeace" were at the heart of protecting the environment, and all plant and animal wildlife that graced the planet. There was no end of support for them, with many of their causes being noble and popular.

With greater exposure and media coverage, this movement in itself, became radicalised and politicised. Greater television coverage of environmental issues, saw Green parties rise in popularity. They began recruiting members through the university campuses, and began attracting left-leaning individuals. Soon, the Greens were a political party that had become a force to be reckoned with, but it was also becoming consumed and overtaken, by anarchists in many countries.

It became less and less concerned with protecting the environment. Instead, the Greens were becoming preoccupied with social issues. Concerningly, they were starting to attract between ten and fifteen percent of the national vote in federal elections. And this vote, being irrelevant in terms of being able to form a government, quickly became a temptation for the left and right, who both needed fifty-one percent of votes or contested seats, to win the right to govern.

The problem confronting the world now, is that the Greens absolutely detest capitalism in all its forms. Their supposed concerns for the planet, are put before the economic needs of the population. Any resource depletion through mining, farming, and fishing, or any development which has an impact on natural resources, is frowned upon.

Likewise, elected Green senators are always pushing a socialist agenda, and are very outspoken, when it comes to any government attempt to stimulate the economy which may adversely impact local ecosystems or local inhabitants. The Greens are radical, and of the extreme hard-left. In Australia, with the Liberal centre-right voters numbering about 51% of the population, the Labor party (around 38%) has had to, somewhat unwillingly, form a coalition with the Greens to try to form government.

This is done through a preferential voting system, which is now seeing society split, virtually fifty-fifty overall, in terms of two-party popularity. Preferential voting systems, see minor political parties allocate their votes to either of the two leading parties (Labor or Liberal), as they concede, that they cannot win a seat or election and govern in their own right.

Preference deals are negotiated prior to elections, with the public made aware of "where" their vote will be directed. Consequently, deals done prior to the election are later honoured, and future policy has to be tailored towards the minority party preferences, in order to be mandated by parliament.

In Australia today, to appease the Greens, the leftist Labor party, is finding itself drawn further to the far-left in terms of its own policies and socialist agenda. The left Labor party, has even lost some of its traditional voters in recent years, as it deserted its "heartland," and decided to pursue more radical agendas and social policy strategies.

Clearly this didn't work for it in the Australian Federal Election of 2019, where Labor lost the "unlosable" election. Common sense prevailed, and capitalism in all its glory (though somewhat declining), continued on its merry way. But for how long, can Australia keep dodging bullets?

4.6 One Nation Party

Aside from the major left and right parties, over the years, many Western nations have had minor parties that represent those who wish to fight for more specific policy issues. Various National parties have also had success, where they emphasise the need for policy that is in the nation's best interest.

One saviour for the Liberals in Australia has been the consistent rise and success of the Independent One Nation Party, founded by Pauline Hanson. Often outspoken, some of her right-leaning policies, have been deemed too controversial for mainstream society and at times, even bordering on racist. However, she has maintained a substantial loyal following, and her preferences have been graciously accepted by the right-leaning Liberals.

Many a Liberal seat has been won, after the combined vote total of the sitting Liberal member, was less than that of the Labor opponent. However, One Nation votes were allocated to the right-leaning Liberals through preference deals, and they go on to win the seat, without winning the populist vote.

Of note here too though, is that as of today, Labor has a bigger similar problem on its hands. It relies on Green preference votes to hold many seats and even then, it can't win the overall majority of seats to govern in its own right. In order to have any chance of governing this nation, Labor has to take the party further and further to the left. Combined with the anarchy and radicalism of the Greens, "a leftist march" through our institutions is now occurring. The Marxists (avid socialism devotees) are becoming more vocal and extreme.

Recent world events such as the covid-19 virus, and the world-wide protests against the "death in police custody" of black American George Floyd, have given the right-of-centre parties, even more impetus regarding nationalism and civil law and order. The One Nation Party was founded upon the notion of Australia first. It has always been highly critical of mass immigration, particularly from China, and also of the sale of our land and assets to foreign nationals or countries. These two events encapsulate the concerns of the Western world at present, and they are at the heart of the greatest conflict facing man and society today.

While the major left and right parties attract all the headlines and majority of votes, the One Nation Party is waging its own little battle against the Greens Party. It is attracting the protest vote of many who have become so disgruntled with the mainstream parties, that they would prefer to place a tick in the "One Nation" box, rather than submit a blank electoral form or even worse, vote for the opposition. So, like its adversary, the Greens, this little party is having a major bearing on election outcomes.

Rising inequality and the global threat of China, have risen to the forefront of everyone's attention. Both of these, are hotly contested issues, and are forcing people to take extremely opposing views on both matters. That is, the left and right are clearly becoming polarised, as policy on the two issues is becoming divisive.

Supporters of each political persuasion are becoming more vocal in professing and supporting their allegiance, and at the same time, are eager to vilify their opponents or anyone who sides with their opposing point of view. This is creating an atmosphere of tension, stirring social unease, and is making the world a much more dangerous place.

Indeed, the "dooms day clock" now sits at 23.57. This metaphoric symbol of "humankind's closeness to man-made catastrophe" has been maintained by members of the Bulletin of the Atomic Sciences since 1947. Midnight, is the hypothetical point at which global catastrophe occurs. Nuclear warfare or global warming were deemed the likely instigators of this. Recent events though, suggest that a pandemic or perhaps even a social revolution, can drastically, alter the course of civilisation. Clearly, political tensions, and a world facing a massive economic collapse courtesy of covid-19, have tipped the free world into uncharted territory.

5

Conflict Within the "Five Eyes."

5.1 Globalisation unifies the battle

"Same horse, different jockey." How many times have we heard that phrase? This globalised world, with its advanced forms of communication and ready access to social platforms, has seen this battle between left and right play out across Western nations. The battle lines are the same. The conflict within each nation is the same. What was once an ideological battle solely contested between nations, is now an issue confronting and dividing members of the same country, state, council, street, household, workplace, and classroom. You cannot escape it.

But how many of our youth have their eyes and minds open to the differing views of the two combatants? Do you rationalise what you see and hear, to formulate your own opinion, or do you "just go with the flow?" Are you voting responsibly and giving your vote the attention that it deserves? Your very livelihood and wellbeing may well soon come to depend on it. Actions have consequences.

What is our youth being taught in the classroom? What are mum and dad doing to explain the differences in political persuasion? Do mum and dad even understand the fundamental differences in principle between the two, themselves? We are being corrupted by what we see and hear. There are now clear agendas that are blatantly obvious within the various forms of media. And it is scary, if you nonchalantly dismiss this, or worse still, if you can't even see it. Virtually every newspaper, television channel, and social platform, has either sided with the left or right. And their virtue signalling has gone from a subtle leaning, to an outright blatant propaganda machination.

To ease the confusion and differentiate between these aligned parties, it is simpler to group the main parties that are always in the news. Daily, our news bulletins generally consist of brief reports on local issues affecting us all. There is, also a portion of the news broadcast, designated to the main news items from the United States of America (our greatest ally), and from the United Kingdom (we are a member of the British Commonwealth). These two nations, plus Australia, Canada, and New Zealand are the five countries that make up the "five eyes" nations. Among them each, the rising conflict between the left and right follows a similar pattern.

For the uninitiated, the left parties (progressives) consist of Labor or ALP (Australia), Labour (U.K.), Labour (New Zealand), Democrats or Liberals (U.S.A) and Liberals (Canada). Their nemesis, the conservatives or right parties, consist of the Liberals (Australia), The Conservatives (U.K.), the National Party (New Zealand), the Republicans (U.S.A), and The Conservatives (Canada). Being the largest parties in their respective countries, periodic elections are generally considered, a "two-horse race" between left and right governance.

All these countries also have in common, a few minor parties, most notably the Greens, who emphasise environmentally and ecologically friendly policy. There are also a few very minor independent parties, who cater for those with far-left or far-right political views.

It is important to expand your own world political knowledge, by understanding the view points of the differing parties. That is, to be able to distinguish left from right. It can get confusing to novice followers of politics, when the Liberals from America (the progressive left), share the same name as the Liberals from Australia (the conservative right), despite being polar opposites. Get this poignant feature right in your head, and you are on your way to fully understanding world politics. When you know the players on your team, cohesion and interplay is much better. So, it is with world politics. Knowing who your Government allies are, from your adversaries, goes a long way towards understanding social and economic forces at play.

Globalisation has made it blatantly obvious that social and economic forces at work in the USA, and the United Kingdom, are playing out in the same manner, here in Australia. The left and right side of politics are becoming polarised everywhere. So much so, that political parties now seem only interested in obtaining or retaining power. Nowadays, important policy measures are rarely delivered by governments of left or right persuasion, successfully or with purpose.

"Paralysis by analysis" is seeing a delay in policy implementation, as the social ramifications and implications of a policy take preference instead. Again, this is leading to frustration from members of society, who are getting fed up with the inaction, and even the incompetence of the major parties. And so, the growing unrest is bubbling to the surface. It is as if the youth, the disgruntled, and the disparaged of today, are seeking a revolution, led by the Marxists (hard-left). They appear on the verge of a rebellion against our regulated society, that had been created through years of growth via capitalism.

Social science statistics (statistical analysis of Census data), point to a deteriorating level of wellbeing among the population. Energy costs are soaring and unemployment is slowly rising. The stress this causes, is leading to a breakdown of the traditional family structure. We are nurturing a generation who have no respect for the basics of right and wrong. Our prisons are so full at present, that newly convicted criminals (of minor misdemeanours), are merely fined or given suspended sentences. Crimes are not being punished through harsh sentencing. The lack of a deterrent is spawning new waves of serious crime.

Even Canada, which has traditionally seen stable progressive governments concentrate on sharing economic gains between all, has seen a rise in the voracity of the right-wing opposition. Recent elections have been fiercely contested, as world affairs are starting to bring a greater awareness of the conflicting political differences.

Left or right is increasingly to the fore, as political campaigns get noisier, dirtier, and very expensive. Today, leading politicians seeking election or re-election, are just as likely to vilify and deride political opponents, as they are to promote new improved policies along party guidelines. It is getting dirty and desperate in this high-stakes political game. Power is everything now, as governing for the people seems to have taken a back seat.

Among this back drop, are the growing levels of personal and national debt throughout the world. This has the potential to bring down the world's economies. Countries seem unable to repay their debts. The burgeoning populations of the world, have seen governments unable to keep up with the health and education demands of the populace.

It used to be said, that "if America sneezes, the rest of the world catches a cold." Not anymore! Today, if America sneezes, the rest of the world says "bless you!" In an instant! Everything is so interconnected, that the World Wide Web (internet), the world stock exchanges, and world financial institutions, react the minute an event of significance takes place. Such is the demand for information and the willingness to make a dollar, or conversely, not lose a dollar.

The Global Financial Crisis of 2008, clearly demonstrated just how precarious the world debt situation really is. The collapse of Lehman Brothers Holding Inc (fourth largest investment bank in The United States), saw world governments injected massive amounts of cash into their financial systems, to prevent a worldwide collapse of financial markets. Most of this money has not been paid back, and it has merely served to further-inflate debt levels.

America, the economic juggernaut of our time, is on the edge of a precipice. It appears to have grown tired of its "world police" role. It has been instrumental in peace-keeping efforts throughout the world since World War Two. It has paid a big price, both in terms of casualties suffered in the combat theatre, and economically, in preserving world stability.

The "Cold War" days of tension with its old adversary, the USSR, seems irrelevant and distant by comparison. The liberation of Kuwait, two Gulf Wars, the defeat of Islamic State (quelling the uprising of the Muslim terrorist outfit ISIS), peace-keeping in Iraq, and economic sanctions against Iran and North Korea, appear to have severely depleted American military forces and the will of the American people.

It seems that growing unequal income distribution is causing issues in mainland America, which are now more urgent than "keeping the peace" in some foreign land. Recent developments have seen the Democrats virtually "declare war" on President Donald Trump, the Republicans, and America at large. The Democrat nominee for the Presidential election in 2020, Joe Biden appears to have lost control of his own Democrat party, as radical leftists have vowed to dismantle capitalism and destroy America as we know it. Frightening times indeed. This does not bode well for traditional allies of America such as Australia.

Large swathes of America are now riddled with debt, rising unemployment, homelessness, and rising racial tensions. Inequality has never been greater. Coincidently, the regions worst affected, are governed locally, by Democrats (the left). There is growing disillusionment with the political systems that have served the country so well for years. People are starting to stand up and speak, demanding to be heard and listened to. Concerningly, only the left can be heard.

Protests, demonstrations, and venting on social media outlets such as Facebook and Twitter, are seemingly spreading the rage like a contagion. Civil disobedience and blatant disregard for the law, is lowering the overall efficacy of "law and order" as we know it. The complainants are forgetful of the fact, that their right to protest only came about, through the sacrifices of those who went before, in protecting the "land of the free."

The means to best address these issues are being debated heatedly. Hence, the current torrid battle within the United States to Govern. The 2016 Election win by Donald Trump of the Republican right, seems to have enraged the "swamp" of ruling class elites from the left.

"Trump Derangement Syndrome" has become rampant in the United States, with the lefty Democrats of America, seemingly intent on destroying greater America, rather than let the Republicans govern with authority and conviction. The defeated Democrats even went as far as trying to "Impeach" President Donald Trump, by falsifying documents to create a "Russian Collusion Hoax." The Federal Bureau of Investigation (FBI), allegedly had members lie in sworn testimony, in an effort to create the illusion that Donald Trump had in fact, won the 2016 election by default. Crazy times. The Democrats were too hypocritical and conceited, to concede that their own Presidential candidate Hillary Clinton, may have cost them precious votes by referring to her fellow Americans as "a basket of deplorables." Mmm. How to make friends and influence people Hillary.

When the "Russian Collusion" bid failed, the left tried for a "Ukraine hoax," again to no avail. Then along came the covid-19 pandemic, where the Democrats tried to blame Trump for the spread of the virus throughout the United States. As usual, they lambasted Trump for not closing the international borders sooner, even though Democrat nominee Joe Biden had stated hypocritically, that he would not have closed the borders. He added, that to do so would have been "xenophobic." That's hypocritical wokeness for you!

Then, as the country went into lockdown and the economy contracted, the left was even encouraging an extension of the lockdown, so as to destroy the economy which was thriving under the Trump administration.

The most poignant thing to remember, is that the vilification of the left and right by each other in America, is now being mimicked in other nations. Especially in the United Kingdom and Australia.

5.2 The Republicans step up in the USA

Following on from the stunning success of Donald Trump in America, there was a new-found reinvigoration in the "passion" of those on the right. The world watched on as Trump Derangement Syndrome gripped the lefties and engulfed American politics. The Democrats were, and still are, despotic in their attempt to remove the duly elected President.

They have been hellbent on vilifying any right-wing policy, and have begun preaching extreme leftist views on their social mediums. This has polarised the nation, one way or the other. While the Democrats want to introduce full socialist reforms, Donald Trump has seen his popularity soar, as his economy goes from strength to strength, on the back of record jobs growth, achieved through removing the impediments to capitalism. The difference could not be greater.

The trickle-down effect of economic growth, (taxes slowly redistributed as social welfare) is infuriating the Democrats. Rising homelessness (mostly in Democratically-governed States), is giving voice to radical socialists who are trying to wrestle control of the Democratic Party.

Donald Trump labelled these socialist leaders and refers to them as "the squad." Their ring leader, Alexandria Ocasio-Cortez, is whipping up her ultra-left base and taking the Democrats to the extreme left. Their fanaticism, while misguided, has served to wake up the sensible, quiet folk who have taken for granted, their personal safety.

Today, Republican rallies are sold out with tens of thousands in attendance, roaring "in approval" of their leader, President Trump. Each of these rallies have proved so popular, that many more thousands are locked out. Who would have thought that politics could be so popular?

In fact, so polarised have the right become, that Donald Trump supporters have taken to wearing his red "Make America Great Again" caps. These are so popular and yet, controversial at the same time. Supporters of the right have been verbally and physically assaulted, just for wearing a Republican cap. But this just tends to inspire them more, in part to antagonise the lefties who are growing more impatient and dangerous, even though they are in opposition. The tension between the two parties, is starting to undo the stability of the country as a whole.

There is a dangerous duality developing, as a result of the polarisation of the left and right. The law is being applied differently to parts of America, governed locally by either Democrat or Republican mayors. For example, certain misdemeanours such as loitering, littering and petty crime now go unpunished by the law in Democrat states. Bail is often not required for minor offenders to be released from police custody in lefty states.

This is a dangerous precedent, which is doing nothing to unify the nation and promote harmony within American society. Law and order are now under threat in America, due to the disregard of the constitution by the progressives. This bears watching, and will require political strength, and the bi-partisan will of the people in years to come, to quell any uprising.

5.3 The United Kingdom steps back from Europe

Buoyed by Republican success in America, in the United Kingdom (UK), the Conservatives have enjoyed resounding success in their own recent battles between left and right. While under the stewardship of the Monarchy and Queen Elizabeth the 2nd, the United Kingdom has been an economic powerhouse, and has enjoyed continued growth, ably directed by a predominantly, two-party parliamentary system.

Margaret Thatcher was a successful Conservative leader from 1979-1990 who took the UK to new heights by encouraging capitalism through deregulation and de-unionising the workforce. So popular and successful was she, that she was dubbed "The Iron Lady." The United Kingdom had seen just how successful a conservative government could be.

Labour took a back seat, until social pressures started to weigh heavily on the British economy. Again, we see that wealth accumulation creates its own form of socialism, to combat rising inequality. This, then necessitates the demand for more wealth, in order to pay for the welfare of those less fortunate. The United Kingdom needed to find bigger markets to quell the insatiable appetite of its populace.

The British left (Labour) under Tony Blair, gained the right to govern in the 1990's, and being ardent supporters of the proposed European Union (EU), they got their mandate to join. On a world stage, greater trade for all of Europe, was supposed to lead to increased wealth for all the countries of the European Union. A greater share of world GDP was a virtuous goal, and so the United Kingdom relented, and joined the Union in search of "a greater share of the spoils."

In 1993, the European Union was formed between 28 European countries. A common currency, a single market, and standardized law throughout Europe, saw economic growth reach new levels, as relatively small countries were able to share in the spoils of international trade. Things were seemingly going well, as travel about the European continent grew rapidly and the dollars followed.

Around the time of the Global Financial Crisis in 2008, things began to turn a little sour for some of the European Union members. Greece and Italy in particular, accrued excessive national debt levels. So much so, that their economies required bailing out by the wealthier members of the EU. This was starting to become a "bit of a drain" on the finances of the wealthier countries such as Great Britain and Germany.

Prior to this, the 9/11 terrorist attacks on America in 2001, had also seen the global threat of terrorism reach new heights. There was unrest in the Muslim world, and resentment of Western civilisation. Some of this was no doubt, jealousy of the West's wealth, better living standards, freedom of speech, and freedom from religious persecution. This led to a deterioration in the stability of the Middle East regions.

Conflict in Afghanistan, saw border skirmishes among neighbouring countries, which required a coalition of Western nations to insert armed forces to keep the peace. Large scale conflicts involving Iran, Iraq, and Syria, and even ethnic cleansing, (disguised as battles of religious ideology), saw millions of people displaced. They all headed for the peace, security, and prosperity of Europe. Disastrously, there was little or no scrutiny of who they were, their skill levels, nor their intentions.

The displaced waves of migrants were quickly drawn to the open borders of the European Union countries. The generous welfare of prosperous nations such as Germany and The United Kingdom made them a prime destination. This was placing a strain on resources. It also served to upset the local population, as the rise in foreigners bought with it, increased crime and racial tension.

Leaders, especially those from the right, were growingly concerned at the negative effect this was having on the local population, especially in terms of rising unemployment and differences in culture. Social tensions were rising. And when they did, the leftist parties were gaining a new found voice.

Jumping to the defence of the often, non-English speaking new arrivals, was seen a means of attracting new voters to a party that has been failing to increase its popularity and voter base. Increasingly, the Labour party were contesting elections, primarily on socialist policies which appease the left base, and which were designed to address any perceived inequalities, be they economic or otherwise.

Conversely, those of the right were adamant that they didn't want to see British economic wellbeing being squandered on social reforms. Open borders were clearly creating a situation where too many people were trying to have "a piece of the pie." There is only so much to go around and inevitably, this would only lead to less for all.

Again, the two-party political system was being tested, and the battle lines between left and right were being "drawn deeper in the sand." In this globalised world, individual nations are still in a race to be the most wealthy and powerful. Buoyed on as their standard of living exceeds that of their neighbours, countries are desperate to maintain and improve economic growth. Financial commitments to, and the open borders of the European Union, were becoming "an albatross around the neck" of the United Kingdom.

The economic progress results are in your face, and published or publicised hourly and daily on news bulletins. The global village had seen the European Union press the United States for economic super power status. But, unfortunately, this Union had its own internal inequalities, with a number of countries not seemingly sharing in the spoils, and others like the United Kingdom, paying too big a price.

In June 2016, after much deliberation, the British Parliament conducted a referendum (public vote) to decide whether the United Kingdom should leave the European Union or remain a member. This was a controversial event that was hotly contested and argued on both sides. Indeed, the voting patterns started to reflect the general political mood of the country.

Those of the right were desperate to leave and the progressives of the left, were hoping to remain. After a startlingly large turnout, those of the right triumphed by 52% to 48%. The British had decided to put the nation first, ahead of the European Union, and had voted to leave. Just how important this was at the time, was yet to be realised.

What followed, was eerily similar to the Trump Derangement Syndrome being witnessed in America. The left did not take the result well at all. General elections were called, seeking a new government to create a mandate to try to overturn the referendum result. Whilst the conservative right had governed since 2010 in Britain, rising socialism was weakening the power of Prime Minister Theresa May. She called a snap general election to try to increase her majority of seats, but only ended up losing more seats. This gave the leftist Labour party renewed vigour, as they sought to delay the "Brexit" (British exit from the EU), with a view to over-turning the Brexit referendum result.

Feeling the threat from the left, the Conservative Party of the right had a spill vote to elect a new leader to the party. Boris Johnson won the vote. He was given the seemingly impossible task of piloting the party, and steering it out of the European Union. The left meanwhile, were becoming more and more vocal in their demands to have a second referendum to try to overturn the first result. They subliminally encouraged social unrest, by condoning and encouraging disharmony in the community.

Labour politicians blocked every attempt by Boris Johnson to leave the Union. They even suggested that polls were indicating that the British people wanted to overturn the result. But polls and the media cannot be trusted, as we shall later see. People were growing tired of this fight among the leaders of both political persuasions. But more importantly, they were sick of seeing their quality of life diminish, while they were "locked-in" to the policies of the Union. Social unrest was increasing, and law and order was under tremendous strain.

Boris Johnson called another snap general election in 2019 to try to increase his Conservative Party's number of seats. He needed a parliamentary majority to complete Brexit. It is here that the battle between left and right, "exploded onto the stage" in the United Kingdom.

Nigel Farage, an extremely popular right-wing politician, formed his own political party, aptly named the "Brexit Party." The sole purpose of its existence was to get Brexit done. An extensive advertising campaign saw its popularity rise quickly. Mr Farage was not seeking to govern in his own right. He was going to preference his received votes to the Conservative Party of Boris Johnson.

The lefty Labour progressives were now led by Jeremy Corbyn, a devout socialist, who had steered the party to the hard-left. His supporters were vocal, radical, extreme, but most of all, confident of victory at the ballot box. They were desperate for socialism to succeed in the United Kingdom. The usual socialist policies of green new deals, open borders, free health care, and free education for all, were trotted out. But most of all, Labour were banking on an election victory to fulfil their wish of staying in the European Union.

What transpired on Thursday, December 12, 2019, will go down in United Kingdom political history. Requiring 326 seats to retain power, the Conservative Party won in a landslide. The greatest electoral victory on British soil since 1970. The margin was 80 seats as the Conservatives won 365 seats in total. Socialism it seemed, was dead and buried. They leftist Labour party were annihilated when it mattered most. The British people had spoken! And with conviction! Those of the right were now gaining ascendency throughout the world. Soon after this election, on January 31, 2020, the United Kingdom formally left the European Union.

Conservative politics it seems, was rising in popularity. Was this about belief in capitalism or was it something else? Is there an increasing fear of socialism starting to rattle the freedom-loving Western world?

5.4 The quiet Aussies speak up down under

Australia, another of the "five eyes," has had a relatively stable political system dominated by the two-party left and right factions. Both sides of the political spectrum were more centrist than extreme, and enjoyed shared success in the 1980's and early 1990's. Firstly, the Labor progressives held government, followed by thirteen years of right Liberal rule under John Howard from 1996-2007.

Financially, Australia, rich in mineral reserves, has been growing rapidly on the back of strong exports of these natural resources. Indeed, many consider the Howard years to being instrumental in driving strong economic growth and giving Australia a "AAA credit rating." But as we continually see, once the dollars flow in, the distribution of them is unequal, and this gives voice to those on the left, eager to share them equitably through welfare.

Capitalising on this, the leftist Labor party regained power during the calamitous Rudd-Gillard-Rudd years of 2007 to 2013. The "time for a change" election result had quickly become an economic disaster for the country. The progressive left was beset by squabbling over leadership and a growing preoccupation with social issues. A wakeup call, as Australians watched all the financial gains of consistent economic growth, being frittered away by a socialist government.

Poor fiscal management of the country, was drastically compounded by Labor government attempts to limit the impact of the Global Financial Crisis in 2008. "Economic Stimulus Packages" proved a disaster. The "pink batts" insulation scheme was rorted and four installers even lost their lives during the debacle. A "building the schools" initiative was undertaken, but mismanaged, and "one off" cash handouts to the public were distributed. National debt levels skyrocketed due to rushed, frivolous, and ill-conceived, government expenditure.

But in typical leftist fashion, the Labor government continued to spend and ran up record debt in record time. And with little regard about how to repay this debt. Of ludicrous note here, was that in 2011, treasurer at the time Wayne Swan, was even the recipient of the "Finance minister of the year" award, issued by the highly regarded "Euromoney" magazine. A crazy decision, looking at the position he put the country into. But it was also a sign of the "craziness" that is now all things "left."

By 2010, the Labor party had lost its way, as Tony Abbott led the Liberal party into a momentous election. Alas, for the first time since 1940, the election resulted in a hung parliament, where neither major party could form government. The nation was evenly divided. The ensuing circus, saw the fate of the nation decided by one elected Green senator and three Independent senators.

They sided with Labor, and Australia was subsequently straddled with three more years of "incompetent" economic mis-management. While the next election couldn't come quick enough, this election result did serve to highlight the growing political power and importance of the Greens, and the Independents too, who had their own ideologies.

The nation was forced to sit through days of grovelling, as the Independents sold their vote to the party that would listen to, and fulfill, their demands. Labour and the Greens, formed a coalition of sorts, and were now "wedded". How ironic, when looking at electoral preference distribution today. History has served us well, so ignore it at your peril. Never has the importance of voting been on better display. Australia had woken up.

The next couple of years saw unrest in Australia, as social causes grabbed the headlines. Economists argued about the best way to address our growing current account deficit. Terrorism was alive and well throughout the world, and the country was divided in its opinion on Australia's role in sending troops to fight overseas.

The Labor party, in its socialist wisdom, had previously decided to open the nation's borders and boy did the boats come. Australia's northern shores were inundated with the arrival of illegal boat people. Asylum seekers setting sail from Indonesia, were arriving in large numbers, and at great expense to the taxpayer.

This quickly became a lucrative little industry for illegal smugglers, who sent unseaworthy boats, overloaded with illegal immigrants, to Australia. These often capsized resulting in many, many hundreds of drownings at sea. This quickly divided the nation between left and right on how to address the problem. The socialists wanted boat people bought safely to shore (on compassionate grounds), while the Liberal voters knew that once they were here, the socialists would fight to keep them here.

Tony Abbott launched his 2013 Liberal (right) election campaign with his signatory policy of "Operation Sovereign Borders." This was to consist of Australian Navy involvement using a boat "turn-back policy" and zero tolerance to illegal boat people. It quickly galvanised those of the right political persuasion, and he was duly elected Prime Minister.

It was such a hotly contested topic, that even the illegal smugglers were waiting on Indonesian shores, listening to transistor radios for news of the election result, just to see if they could resume "plying their trade." The relief was palpable, as the boats more or less, stopped straight away. The Labor party were left to "whinge and whine" about the social injustice of this, and the lack of compassion that those of the right had come to display. Or was this once again, dismay and recognition of the fact that, they couldn't increase their future voting base?

The Liberals, under Tony Abbott, once again undertook the onerous task of reinstalling responsible fiscal management to "reign in" the rising debt levels. Spending was tightened, to the frustration of the left, while impediments to business growth were relaxed. Once again, the economy was on the move, although social forces around the world were starting to influence political decision making more and more.

The rise of Facebook, the use of Twitter, and emerging bias among media outlets, were all instrumental in exposing social injustice and inequity throughout the world. Virtue signalling became trendy and started to drive a wedge in society, as opinion was split on virtually every issue that developed. The ability to implement government policy, was stifled by opposition from the left and the minority independents, who used socialist excuses not to pursue capitalist objectives. Australia was not immune to this.

This was always narrowing the "preferred Prime Minister" poll numbers and the "preferred party" polls. The Success of Tony Abbott in stopping the boats, was being pegged back on other socialist issues, and he was soon behind in the polls. Pouncing on this, Malcolm Turnbull initiated a spill against the sitting Prime Minister in 2015, and Tony Abbott was forced to relinquish his prized role.

Concerningly for the Liberals, was that while Mr Turnbull was seen as a fine orator and master of economic strategy, he also had leftist leanings. He always denied that he wanted to lead Labor, yet many a Labor politician, will readily admit that Mr Turnbull had approached the Labor party about joining them in the mid 1990's. Regardless of this, he had accomplished his "selfish" goal of becoming Prime Minister of Australia.

The warning signs had been there. In the Mid 1990's, Mr Turnbull was a leading figure in forming the Republican Party. Their sole objective was to take Australia out of the Commonwealth, and this ignited heated debate "down under." A referendum on this issue was held in 1996, with the no/remain vote succeeding, thereby thwarting this egotistical man's desire to be Australia's first President. But it did thrust him into the "political spotlight," and it had given a hint about his leftist, socialist leanings.

Seemingly not interested in keeping the Liberals ahead of the chasing lefties in the polls, Mr Turnbull directed his and Liberal Party attention, to the new growth industry of renewable energy. The world has become fixated on the threat of global warming, and Mr Turnbull realigned traditional policies to address this issue. This was to appease the masses, and although he re-iterated that he was for the sensible centre, senior Liberal figure heads were concerned that the party was now lurching towards the left, under the stewardship of Malcolm Turnbull.

The Liberals held onto government in the 2016 general election under Turnbull, winning by the narrowest margin of one seat. There was agitation in the ranks, as Mr Turnbull was taking the Liberals too close to the left, upsetting the base of the party.

This was at a time when those of the left were becoming more radical and vocal, as they used global warming as a means to increase their socialist base. Having been signed up to the Paris Agreement (where nations commit to cut carbon emissions), the economy was starting to wilt under the growing cost of implementing renewable forms of energy generation. Liberal concern at falling poll figures was again on the rise.

But Mr Turnbull could not be told. His socialistic tendencies were once again on display, when his government wilted on the matter of same-sex marriage. Wokeness had seen the debate for same sex-marriage around the world, grow louder by the day. Despite being warned that this legislation may "open a can of worms," Malcolm Turnbull led the implementation of a referendum on the matter.

In 2017, the "yes" vote prevailed and same-sex marriage was passed into law. This had all sorts of ramifications, especially for the church and religion. It also spawned the growth of the "LGBT" movement. A minority group of Lesbian, Gay, Bi-sexual, and Transgender folk, now had untold power, and they ran with it. Socialism had "grown another leg" through its new found voice.

Combined with a desire to be politically correct and woke at all costs, every conceivable social issue was gaining widespread support, most noticeably from the left. Freedom of speech was in danger too, as the socialists set about planning dangerous and expensive reforms.

Every event of significance, was being politicised one way or the other (left or right). Labor was ahead in the pre-election polls and very confident at the pending 2019 general election. So much so, that they put forward their agenda of growth-destroying policy, which would see wealth redistributed to the public sector. Higher taxes were promised, along with a plan to "go green," by setting a target of 50% renewable energy provision. Those of the right were terrified, as were many in society, at this plan which was bordering on "an economic suicide note."

Labor Treasurer at the time Chris Bowen, was so confident and forthright, that in one press conference, discussing changes that would adversely affect pensioners, he arrogantly boasted "if you don't like our policy, then don't vote for us." Just as Hillary Clinton had insulted the American voters, the leading left figures of Australia had become arrogant beyond belief, and certainly "on the nose."

Labor Leader Bill Shorten, was so confident of moving into the lodge as Prime Minister, that he began packing up his belongings before the election. The media considered the result a foregone conclusion, and were readying their "Liberals Defeated" headlines. Even the Liberals knew "the writing was on the wall." They were getting smashed now in the polls and heading towards a landslide defeat. It was a case of "desperate times call for desperate measures."

In the months preceding the 2019 election, the Liberals initiated a "spill" against sitting Prime Minister Malcolm Turnbull. Forty-eight hours of chaotic backroom deals ensued, in an effort to insert Peter Dutton as new Prime Minister. This created deep divisions amongst the Liberal party members. Mr Turnbull had taken the party too far to the left, and there would be disastrous repercussions for Australia, if Labor should happen to win the election. At least Mr Dutton, who had been a key minister in stopping the boats, had a greater aversion to the right. He was viewed as being able to possibly limit collateral damage at the polls.

But Mr Turnbull tried every conceivable trick in the book to remain in office. He evoked little known constitutional laws and ordered a recount. This time, Mr Dutton didn't have the numbers due to last minute, secret backroom deals. But neither did Malcolm Turnbull. The spill result was announced to the waiting media masses, and Scott Morrison was thrust forward, to be installed as Prime Minister. It seemed to matter little. There was so little time to go before the election, that he was deemed "a lamb to the slaughter."

A humble man of religion and the centre-right, the capitalist hopes of a nation, were now riding on his shoulders. All the while, the socialist left basked in the glory of impending control of Government. Even the Greens were more forthright than ever, as their social "utopia" dreams took a step closer to becoming reality. Preference deals were done between the Greens and Labor, promising socialist reform like never before.

Only a miracle could save the conservative Liberals from losing power in Australia. The independent One Nation Party was still flying its nationalistic flag in its policy offerings, especially on excessive immigration levels, and the growing threat of China. The newly formed Independent Clive Palmer Party, also spent a fortune on advertising "the dangers to all things Australian," if Labor were to win the election.

All their preferences were to flow to the Liberal Party and would be sorely needed. Scott Morrison was a simple man, with the simple slogan of "jobs and growth." The tried and tested formula of right-leaning governments.

Thankfully, another glimmer of hope among right voters, was the fact that Labor was banking on preferences of the Greens to get elected. Alas, Labor leader Bill Shorten, in making pre-election deals with the Greens, had promised heavy carbon emission reductions. This meant the abandonment of mining, and certainly preventing the opening of the Adani mine in Queensland.

In essence, this was "a kick in the face" to traditional, unionised Labor voters. Combined with taxing pensioners more, Labor had seemingly, "turned its back" on its traditional heartland, as it set about chasing extra socialist votes.

May 18, 2019, will go down in history as one of the most dramatic days in Australian political history. Scott Morrison was retained as Prime Minister at the general election, and had increased the number of Liberal seats in parliament. Bill Shorten had lost "the unlosable election" and by a significant margin. Scott Morrison, when making his victory speech in front of his delirious voters, summed it up best when he said "the quiet Australian voters have spoken." Against the odds, against the predictive, pre-election polling trends, amid a symphony of boisterous Labor and Green oratory fanaticism, and against a baying anti-right media horde, the right had prevailed.

Like the election of American President Donald Trump, Brexit, and the landslide win of Boris Johnson in the United Kingdom, the political "right" had triumphed, and retained the right to govern. Capitalism for the meantime was safe, despite the growing consensus, that socialism is on the rise and appears inevitable.

The mainstream media had sided with the left around the world, and now appear to be leading the fight everywhere, to have those of the right removed from power. Australia had dodged a bullet and won the battle, but the war is far from over. Understanding the difference between left and right has never been more important.

5.5 Canada squeezes the life out of the left

A relatively stable and quiet member of the "five eyes," Canada has enjoyed a fruitful existence, and is considered a peace-loving nation. Canada has a multi-party parliamentary system that is considered to be fully democratic, where there is an emphasis on equality and inclusiveness for all its people.

Despite peace, order, good-will, and social justice being the goal, Canadian politics is still dominated by the two traditional parties of the left (the Liberals), and the right (Conservatives). There are also three other minor parties who attract a lot of support. They are the New Democrats (currently holding 24 seats), Bloc Quebecois (32 seats), the Greens (3 seats), and one Independent.

To govern in Canada however, you need a majority of 170 seats out of the 338 that are contested. Canada has a tradition of progressivism and moderate centrist political ideology. Far-left or far-right political persuasion has never been prominent in Canadian society, and is a major reason why recent electoral history, has reflected patterns seen elsewhere around the Western world.

Canada has always been a staunch ally of the Western nations and has enjoyed similar economic growth and development. With the growth in support for socialism, it too, has endured increasing pressure on its population to meet Paris Agreement Targets. Green energy is expensive, and there is a growing resentment of these costs being thrust upon the local population.

Despite saturation media coverage of socialist issues, the recent 2019 Canadian general election, played out in a similar fashion to those of the USA, the UK, and Australia. Justin Trudeau (a noted environmentalist), was the leader of the Liberals (left), who held a majority (170 seats) prior to the election. The Liberals just managed to hold on at the election, but were reduced to a minority government holding only 157 seats, just ahead of the Conservatives on 121 seats. This was the second worst performance by a political party in Canadian history, as they only won 35% of the popular vote. This was also the lowest percentage of national popular vote of a governing party in Canadian history.

Once again, the quiet people had spoken. There was a massive shift to the political right. What phenomenon is at work, that is creating this shift to the right around the world? And why is it happening, despite the growing activism and parochialism of those of the left? It seems to me, that there is more of an inherent understanding by the population of the differences between the two political ideologies, than we first thought. Is it the experience of our older voters, that is creating this momentum?

Of concern, when looking at the age and energy level of the leftist activists on media coverage of all things political, are our younger voters going to arrest or maintain this momentum in years to come? Do they fully understand the ideology of the political combatants? How long can Western nations continue to fight to hold onto their economic gains, before they are "prostituted away" on often frivolous socialist policies? And what is driving this widening gap between left and right?

5.6 The conservatives retain plurality in New Zealand

New Zealand, like Australia, is a Constitutional Monarchy with Queen Elizabeth the 2nd, as the Head of State. It has a multi-party parliament, but with two major parties, the Labour Party (left) and The Nationals (right). Throughout history, there has been an emphasis on social welfare and multiculturalism in New Zealand. This has led to a suppression of far-right politics, and resulted in closely fought elections, as a large majority of the population sits in the sensible centre.

A peace-loving nation, it ranks highly on government transparency, and is perceived to have the lowest level of corruption in the world. In the 1930's and 1940's, Labour governments built up the New Zealand economy, on the back of investment in the public sector, mainly through increased unionism, generous social welfare, and by undertaking public works. Alternate National governments, then set about removing impediments to free enterprise, and containing welfare spending without dismantling it. Since 1970, the country has taken on a more Liberal outlook (left).

Of note, New Zealand signalled these intensions in the 1980's. It was at the forefront of the battle for nuclear disarmament. World attention was drawn to New Zealand in 1985, when the Greenpeace flagship "Rainbow Warrior," was sunk in Auckland Harbour by two Secret Intelligence French Operatives. The Government passed legislation thereafter in 1987, to make New Zealand a nuclear-free zone, where nuclear-powered ships were no longer allowed into New Zealand ports. It thereby, had to forgo its place in the "ANZUS alliance," which was formerly, a treaty (ratified in 1951) between Australia, New Zealand, and the United States, guaranteeing armed support in times of conflict. Times were changing.

In recent years, the Government was also instrumental in protecting the rights of the LGBT society. (Lesbians, Gays, Bi-sexual, and Transgender folk). It also legalised same-sex marriage, and recently, legalised abortion. Protecting the rights of the local indigenous Maori party, has also been a prerogative of governing parties, although this was often contentious, and always ensured minor parties got plenty of votes.

Indeed, social injustice has spawned the rise of many minor parties such as The Greens, The Maori Party, the Progressive Party, New Zealand First, and the United Future Party. Such a spread of voting choices has seen closely fought elections, where neither major party can win enough seats to govern effectively, through holding a majority of seats in parliament.

As shown, despite New Zealand being relatively small, it has been pioneering on many controversial issues, where the socialist left has been making more and more noise in recent years. At the 2017 general election, the Nationals had been in power since 2008. Would the momentum towards the right, on display around the world, be maintained in New Zealand? Well just like Canada, the election proved to be very tight. So much so, that neither Labour nor the National Party won enough seats to form a minority government.

Noticeably, the Nationals (right) retained their plurality (won more votes than anybody else) in the House of Representatives, but could not form government as they lacked a majority of seats. Jacinda Ardern, leader of the Labour party, was later able to form a coalition with the New Zealand First party, and the leftist Labour party was back in office after nine years in opposition.

How this plays out remains to be seen, but there was frustration and dislike of the whole coalition-forming process. It alienated a lot of voters. Today, New Zealand appears to be heading down the socialist left path, where the growing resentment of this can be seen in the rhetoric of the right. Indeed, Jacinda Ardern with her socialist policy, is "on the nose" with many in New Zealand.

Once again, there appears to be a leaning overall, to the right. Why is this, and at a time when the left has never been more vocal? The left is receiving favourable support in media circles. They have tended to be the most popular in polling between elections, and yet they have had disastrous results at elections in many countries. Fortuitously, at present, there is a growing level of support for the right political persuasion in other countries such as Germany, France and Hungary as well.

6
The Rising Threat of Socialism

6.1 A sense of inevitability?

Early chapters, have highlighted the significance of economic growth in laying the foundation for political success, achieved by right-leaning governments around the world. However, we also briefly touched on the forces that have given the socialist movement its strength in recent years. Why has this not led to electoral success?

Let it be clear from the outset, that all Western nations have all had their share of successful left-leaning governments. This was the will of the people at times, and what was considered to be best for a nation. It is as if, that as the economy grew and wealth was accumulated, eventually the left would come into power, and through more generous spending, they would redistribute this quicker than their capitalist government counterparts. Historically, cyclical election results of the "five eyes" nations over the last century, are testimony to this.

These nations have all prospered enormously, and have consistently, had relatively low levels of unemployment and poverty. They also have high living standards, enjoy fantastic health and education standards, are protected by a strong military, and have a well-adjusted system of law and order. All evidence, that there is clearly room for socialism and capitalism in society at the same time.

Afterall, there is only one better system of government than full democracy. Unfortunately, on planet earth, with its multitude of differing cultures, religions, and ethnicities, perfect government is impossible to achieve. An "unattainable utopia" if you like. "Self-governance" is the dream scenario where everyone is free, trusted, and able to interact peacefully with everyone around them, and without infringing on the inherent rights of others. Sounds good, but the battle to achieve this, has been waged unsuccessfully since the dawn of time.

6.2 Marxism

In the nineteen century, Karl Marx put forward his economic and political theories, to rationalise the socio-economic phenomena that were shaping different nations. It was a simple philosophy, analysing the material condition and economic activity required to fulfil human material needs. Clearly, he was onto something, which bears mentioning, given the state of society today.

Marxism, assumes a country's form of economic organisation (means of production) influences all other social phenomena. In essence, the minority own the means of production (the bourgeoisie), whilst the vast majority of the population, actually produce the goods and services (proletariat). It is here, that socio-economic analysis, recognises the struggle between the different social classes.

As we have seen, capitalism has increased the means of production, through technological advances which then increase productivity levels. However, this has displaced workers who can no longer share in the wealth creation, and they soon find themselves sliding down the classes, as they become reliant on social welfare. The Marxists view capitalism as unsustainable, as nations can no longer continually improve living standards for the whole population. As wages fall, the ability to generate taxes to finance social spending, also diminishes.

Those in power or the elite, then spend excessively on defence or their military, either individually or as a nation, to protect their hold on power. By further heightening of the gulf in classes, socialism then rises through revolution. Socialism gains its strength by satisfying human needs, rather than creating private profits. Marxists believe that this rise in socialism is not an inevitability, but a necessity. Is this what we are witnessing in society today? Do we have anything to fear? "You bet your bottom dollar we do!"

Marxism has had a profound effect on global academia. History, the arts, anthropology, media, science, theatre, sociology, cultural studies, education, economics, ethics, criminology, geography, psychology, and philosophy, have all been in the news as they come under attack from the left. Today, it seems that each of these, has been politicized one way or another, to support the arguments of the left. Are we merely watching this Marxism phenomenon continually play out, as the capitalism-driven economies correct themselves, and concede ground to the socialists?

If this is the case, why has the social revolution become so volatile? What else has happened to create this social unease that has made the world a dangerous place? Why are people of differing political persuasions becoming so polarised? Impatience with, and ignorance of one another, has grown to dangerous levels. Tolerance of opposing views has never been so low.

Just like the Brexit fracture in the European Union, and the recent election results in the "five eyes" countries, on a domestic level, all countries are now facing a similar crisis internally. Disgruntled sections of local populations are gradually finding a voice, and starting to protest at the rising inequality between the wealthy and not-so-fortunate within their own communities. It is this conflict which has manifested itself in a full-blown culture war.

The woke brigade are instigating this battle. Whether deliberately or inadvertently, they are hijacking every little significant event or topic of discussion, and weaponizing it. The rise in voice of the perceived minorities, is countered by the argument from those of the right, who have heeded the lessons from history. Socialism, and its policy of sharing wealth evenly throughout the whole community, has failed repeatedly.

While socialism occasionally gains a foot hold in societies, it has never been able to dominate political persuasion for too long. Protracted socialism has throughout time, eroded the minority domination of wealth by the elites at the top, to such an extent, that it leads to dictatorship and eventually communism. History has shown this, and it is never a pleasant outcome. Wellbeing diminishes, freedom of speech disappears, and non-compliance to the state rules, often results in death. World Wars have been fought and won, to prevent this from reoccurring.

Today, Venezuela is living testimony to all that is wrong with the leftist philosophy. Socialist policy has seen it on the verge of collapse. Massive fortunes were acquired through Venezuela's exportation of oil, which was extracted from its abundant natural reserves. Meanwhile as the spoils were not shared evenly, high unemployment in other sectors, led to the falling individual wealth of many. Society has collapsed here, with rampant poverty, a health system unable to cater for a large population, declining education standards, and shortages of food, ruining the nation's overall standard of living.

Social unrest is compounded, by resentment at the political corruption of the government, which is trying to retain power and resist any attempts to overthrow it. The presiding government is holding onto power, despite being undemocratically elected. The government has had to use military force to control the local population. Nice!

Venezuela was once a great oil producer, and rich in natural resources, which created its early wealth. The world watched on as it became a "shining example" of how to share the wealth of a country among its population. Alas, it has now become an example of how "socialism has failed."

What seems an honourable plan for society to share equally, has repeatedly failed, as the people of Cuba and other nations will also testify. Yet, why are the lessons not being heeded? Why is there a desire to follow a flawed, repeatedly proven, doomed economic plan and system of government? At the end of the day, Venezuela is living proof that "you can't make the poor rich, by making the rich poor."

Why is there now a fanatical argument against capitalism, and all the benefits that it has been shown to bring? The answer lies in a close examination of how "wokeness" has invaded every aspect of society. Technological advances in communication have seen personal opinions (often thought about, but rarely expressed or spoken) now become a topic of global conversation (especially through the advent of Twitter). The story is the same everywhere you go, as we have become a global village.

While Marxism can explain what is happening, and can account for the correcting of wealth distribution and societal attempts to restore equality, there is more to the growing dangers of this obsession with all things socialist, and the danger they represent.

6.3 The hurdle confronting the left

It is all very well evaluating current national affairs on the natural, cyclical redistribution of wealth through public service provision and welfare. This is a universal progression of societal development, and ensures that the less fortunate, share in the economic growth driving the rises in GDP.

It is instrumental in nurturing peace, stability and social cohesion, and has the support of everyone, regardless of their political persuasion. The problem facing society today though, is that there is "no pie" left to share. As we have seen, the Global Financial Crisis in 2008, saw governments inject vast sums of money into their financial systems, to prevent a collapse of the banking system.

Leading governments are now in debt, "to the tune" of many billions or trillions of dollars. And this, is a debt that has to be repaid, for countries to retain their sovereignty and future stability. Political battles are now being fought on the policies, and ability, to address and repay this debt. The right is emphasising the need for profit-making economic growth, while the left is distracted by social causes, and prefers to offer green solutions, to address the debt and climate issues simultaneously.

The "clock is ticking" and as yet, none of the Western nations have been able to arrest their spiralling debt. As we move forward, this burden is going to be met in the future, by the younger generations. With rising personal living, health, and education costs, and with declining housing affordability and standards of living, young individuals already have enough to contend with.

This is also at a time and age when they are extremely impressionable. They are all consumed by the internet, and the advent of the "iPhone," has seen them interconnected like never before. With this, there is growing concern that they are being bombarded with socialist propaganda, which is inciting hatred towards the cause of their current predicament. They are being urged to rise up against the capitalist system that is "supposedly," suppressing their ability to get ahead in life. There is a growing consensus, that they have given up on the great Australian dream of home ownership.

Watch any protest march, and you will see, that the young are now at the front and centre. They are also spending more time at university, seeking an edge in their qualifications, which will enable them to find meaningful employment in the future. But this just drives up their personal debt levels as well. It is as if every individual, as well as every country, is drowning in debt. This does not bode well, for those in need of social welfare in the years to come.

The 2019/20 covid-19 pandemic, which emanated out of China, has drawn attention to this calamitous situation. To prevent the spread of the virus, countries closed their borders and isolated their populations. This had the adverse impact, of effectively, closing down their respective economies. Unemployment has skyrocketed, and all nations have gone into a recession. This "once in a lifetime" event, has distorted markets to a level never seen before. Experts are divided in their opinion, as to how and when the world will get itself out of this mess.

One thing is for sure. Economies are in more trouble than ever before. In Australia for example, at the height of the pandemic in early 2020, 72% of the population were either employed in the public sector, or in receipt of some sort of social welfare. The traditionally, more productive, private sector was shrinking. Further, excessive rules, red tape, and regulations were stifling the ability of entrepreneurs to open or return to growing their businesses.

The economy, now in recession, has even less means with which to finance social welfare for an ever-growing population. Australian Government attempts to stimulate growth through policy initiatives such as "homebuilder," and to support the newly unemployed through benefits such as "jobseeker" and "jobkeeper," have only served to further increase the national debt levels by over $80 billion.

One thing is for sure, socialism is not a stable, reliable political system of government, when there is "no pie" from which to draw funds. With no government surpluses created, ongoing and deepening national debt, and growing inequality between the elites and lower classes, something has to give. Have we reached this point, where the left, rather than have their hands out, are now rebelling, and seeking to destroy that which has been created and accumulated over the years? Is their petulance, a sign that they are angry that there is "no more easy money" for them? It certainly would seem so.

6.4 Two peas in a pod

There are two words which should be on "tip of everyone's tongue," but they are rarely mentioned. The "two peas in a pod!" (2P's); "Ponzi," and the other concern "Paris." Both of these should concern us, because they can "upset the apple cart at any time."

Charles Ponzi, inadvertently alerted the world to white collar crime in the 1920's, by creating a fraudulent "Ponzi scheme." This bloke made a small fortune, by luring investors into his scheme, on the promise of strong profits with little risk. However, he paid himself and also the other early investors handsomely, with funds deposited by the newest investors. The early investors are duped into believing the great returns are from solid sales.

This system works in the short term, and tricks investors into believing in the ongoing success of their investment. As long as there are new investors, the illusion is maintained, and the instigator of the scheme makes a fortune. But the scheme crashes when there are no more investors, no sales exist, and the newest investors want their share of the profit. They ended up losing all their money except for Charles.

Does this remind you of anything? The GFC of 2008, is the closest the world has come to suffering a similar fate. Banks rely on taking deposits from customers, and then lending out the funds to borrowers. They make an absolute fortune in the process. However, they are then liable for all the debts of their customers. The GFC got the Lehman's financial institution into trouble, because they had so much debt, that they could not repay simultaneously, the deposits of all their customers. Customers rushed the bank to get their money out, but the money wasn't there anymore. They needed a government bailout to prevent a worldwide crash of banking.

When one bank fails, they can fall like dominoes, such is their dependence on one another. This is a scary proposition, given the covid-19 pandemic, and the massive recession the world is currently facing. With property prices sliding again, and personal debt at record levels, how long before we see another collapse of the banking system?

While the banks operate similar to a Ponzi scheme (but are regulated by government), there is another Ponzi scheme pushed onto society by our political leaders, regardless of their political persuasion. Economic growth works in much the same fashion, in that it relies on population growth to boost GDP levels of countries.

A higher population through immigration, can boost spending and taxation revenue, even if this raises government spending on service provision in the interim. Spending has a multiplier effect. Money paid as wages or in the form of social welfare, is rarely saved. Most is spent on goods and services, which drives up the profits, and then the spending of other individuals and entities. Over and over. Give an unemployed person an allowance of $300 a week, and that money is soon in the hands of other members of society. The $300 multiplies in value.

Eventually, overall wealth rises and with that, property prices march ever onwards and upwards. The economic growth figures then make the politicians in charge, seem highly re-electable. However, over time, cities become incredibly crowded, and the demand for transport, health, and education services, soon exceeds supply. This reduces overall quality of life, and places pressure on governments to limit immigration numbers.

The problem with this though, is that with no new money from increased population numbers, economic growth stagnates, just like the profits in the Ponzi model. Just as the newest investors lose their money, economic growth requires continued immigration or rising natural birth levels, to stimulate the demand needed to prevent the collapse of the system. The lack of perpetuation in growth sees asset prices crash and debt levels soar.

In Australia, there was heat on ministers to slow immigration due to these socioeconomic forces, well before the covid-19 virus struck Australian shores. The indefinite closed borders, will have a drastic effect on the ability of the government to sustain economic growth. Retreating property prices, soaring unemployment, and massive personal debt levels, are pointing to an economic Armageddon.

No one wants to talk about this, as leading government ministers "tiptoe" around the "recession" word. Maybe, this is why the socialists are upset. "If you see the bandwagon it's too late. You had to be on it." Has the serious money already been made? Are the newest to the market about to lose a fortune? Will society collapse in an economic Ponzi-style collapse? Of note here, the Ponzi scheme is like a pyramid, with the wealth accrued at the top, and little else trickling down to an ever-increasing base.

Funny how the world at the moment, has a lot of wealth shared by an elite few at the top of the tree, while the number of "have nots" is growing ever large. This bears thought!

The second "P" word that should be "flavour of the month" is "Paris," as in "Paris Agreement." Whilst we all know what this agreement refers to, we need to pay special attention to the hypocrisy surrounding it. This agreement, is also at the heart of the battle of left versus right. It is noble and wise to address any concerns regarding the impact of human behaviour on the environment.

But it is highly illogical, to not administer the binding agreements and legislation of this Agreement, fairly and equitably, amongst the nations who have signed up for the recommended policies. Some countries have to do much more "heavy lifting" to meet their Paris targets. Others spend an absolute fortune trying to implement renewable energy, while others still, such as America, have pulled out of the Agreement altogether. Australia is closing coal-fired power stations, while China is building hundreds of them. How is that fair all you socialists? Isn't equality the cornerstone of socialism? Why are the socialists not denigrating China in the same manner they vilify people for not being "woke?"

The socialist lefties are quick to embrace wokeness when it suits them. Why then, do they also embrace the Paris Agreement, and refute any arguments to withdraw from the agreement? Pretty hypocritical to be woke, and yet not call out the behaviour of China.

Or is it because once again, they are using the Agreement as a form of wealth redistribution between the "well-to-do" and the "less-fortunate?" Is the Paris Agreement, a tool to "attack the conscience" of the West? And as for these faceless keyboard warriors, are they dominated by the Chinese? The Chinese want to infiltrate the West. Are the architects of "wokeness," in fact, the Chinese themselves? Or is the Chinese Communist Party financing the anarchists, in an attempt to destroy the West from within? Is wokeness just another trojan horse?

Worse still! Has the United Nations been bought by the Chinese too? It seems the freedom-loving people of Hong Kong, The World Health Organisation, The United Nations, and the introduction of the covid-19 virus into the Western world, all have something in common. I wonder what that could be? By now, you should know the answer. If I disappear, you will definitely know the answer!

The conservatives are now fighting on two fronts. While we are now economically vulnerable, we have to confront the aggression on our doorstep from China, as well as the rowdy lefties inside our borders. Not to mention the covid-19 virus. Interesting times. While the left "mob" is marching through our institutions, determined to change the world, are we reaching the point where socialism morphs into communism?

6.5 The rise of the mob

Conflict is described as a serious, protracted, disagreement over principles, feelings, opinions or interests. Put more simply, it is a battle between the "haves" and the "have nots." Clearly the "have nots" when it comes to wealth, massively outnumber the "haves." So much so, that the top five percent of the richest people on the planet, control ninety-five percent of the total money on the planet.

The beneficiaries of this economic growth are very small in number, and the benefits are not evenly distributed. Is it this that has driven the animosity between those of the left and the right? Is the dismay from the wealthy, who are angry at losing what they have, or from the less-fortunate, desperate to take what they don't have? Or both? Regardless of which, the resentment from the "have nots" is growing to dangerous levels.

I give you the musicians. "I work all night, I work all day, to pay the bills I have to pay... ain't it sad!" ABBA were right when they said it's all about "money, money, money!" Jimi Hendrix was spot on too when he said, "when the power of love overcomes the love of power, the world will know peace." A dangerous obsession borne out of necessity, is looming.

Even sensible centre-left political persuasion, is under threat itself from the mob. The far-left activists, antifa, anarchists, and radicals, have hijacked the many "left-of-centre" parties right around the world. So much so, that leaders of left parties now seemingly endorse their antics, as they need their votes to bolster chances of electoral success. That's right, they condone the extremist behaviour, purely because they value their votes more. This is lunacy.

The current education system, riddled with lefty ideology, has spawned a generation of "trojan horse jockeys." These folks do not fit into society as we know it. They have, in their dangerous, mischievous hands, the "reigns of the bandwagon that steers the lefty narrative." Our young are being taught to hate themselves, hate their country, hate Western civilisation, and to think that free speech and debate is wrong. The LGBT mob enhance this, by saying that all men are potential rapists, that there are no biological genders, and that socialism and communism, are the only way forward. More lunacy that is not being denounced.

The left now proclaims that the only way to get your point across, is through non-conformity, abuse, and violence. A lot of bright young people are being brainwashed, filled with hate, and are throwing their hard-earnt intelligence away because of it. They are making themselves heard, but are destroying the source of their privilege at the same time.

This "insane" agenda has been invented by the politics of the left, and worse still, is being supported by tax payers money. Pounded into submission by being called racist, sexist, xenophobic, homophobic, and numerous other "isms," the "truth" is being replaced by appropriate "lies."

The media and social mediums, are willing co-conspirators, in this build-up of hatred towards capitalism and those of the right. The mob have become dangerous and embraced a "pack mentality" to take down one by one, any individual, company or political party that stands in their way. At the time of writing, the law seems powerless to stop them. Individuals and politicians are often unwilling to denounce their actions and behaviour, for fear of retribution.

7

Understanding Humanity

7.1 Knowing the opposition

It is readily apparent today, that minds are split on the virtues of left versus right. The precarious balancing act of all governments to service the needs of the population, in a fiscally prudent manner, is more perilous with massive debt levels. The need to understand the differing systems of government is vital, for future voters to have confidence in the longevity of the society they inhabit.

That said, what are individual human traits of us all, that complicate our behaviour and contribute to the animosity that we see today? These traits need to be acknowledged by political parties, as they seek to secure and enhance their voter base. It is wise to know your enemy or in the political spectrum, know what your opponent stands for.

Being able to gauge the mood and wellbeing of general society, can ensure that policy settings serve the whole population, and not just certain minority groups. Afterall, whenever a new government is elected, leaders are quick to acknowledge their Party supporters, but just as quick, to assure opposition voters that they are in power to govern for all, and not just the victorious.

7.2 Anatomy

We are all unique individuals, and no two humans share identical Deoxyribose Nucleic Acid (DNA). Yet despite this, regardless of our nationality, skin colour, culture, or religious belief, our needs are all relatively simple and similar. We all instinctively seek peace, happiness, warmth, shelter, and food in order to grow. An obvious noble and common goal. As a species we are all born with the same anatomy and ability to develop, except for a misfortunate few, who are mentally or physically handicapped. Our brains are wired to protect us by avoiding pain, and also to preserve the sanctity of life.

However, it seems that geography has an understated bearing on our respective development. Our rate of learning (education) through tuition, and adherence to differing religious beliefs and cultures, does create differences among us. We acquire differing levels of wealth, and endure unique experiences, which give us all different perspectives of the world.

But "wise heads prevail," and we have learnt to share and coexist peacefully. We have taken "pride" in our accomplishments. Clearly though, some are more fortunate than others. A small minority have even accumulated extravagant wealth running into the billions of dollars ("gluttony"). Good luck to them.

In the battle of the sexes, it is commonly agreed "the men shall hunt and the women shall gather." This is in our DNA, regardless of how we feel. Families and communities have thrived, as we all live in an orderly fashion in households, villages, towns, cities, and countries. Men have traditionally, financially supported their families, while the women have raised the children and made the home. Through the church and religious teachings, the nuclear family (married parents and their dependents) was seen as a stabilising and desirable goal, for individuals and society alike.

In recent years, the prominent LGBT movement has frowned upon this stereo-typed notion, and has encouraged changes to certain laws, in order to promote equality for all sexualities. Condoning and permitting same-sex marriage, is an obvious example of their rejection of the traditional nuclear family.

Things are changing rapidly. An obsession with equality (wokeness) has turned everything, seemingly, on its head. Minorities of every persuasion are demanding to be heard. Against this backdrop, political parties that regulate, monitor, and develop our societies, have become increasingly obsessed with retaining or acquiring power (if they are in opposition). We are seeing selfish individual and collective behaviour, that is detrimental to our overall societal wellbeing.

This is human nature. As individuals we all "covet." We want things that we see that can make our lives better, but which are often unattainable, due to our circumstance. This can quickly create "jealousy" and "envy," which can result in negative behaviour towards those who have what we want. This certainly explains "Trump Derangement Syndrome."

It is an urge, chemically manifested in our brains, which then controls our emotions and actions. We all remember being little kids and not having the newest trendy toy that our friends had. We would "spit the dummy," and have a tantrum until we got our way.

"Greed" and "lust" are derived from "covet." They are extremes of human behaviour. Is it these natural phenomena that are driving political parties to the hard-left or hard-right? There is no doubt, that the left is being overtaken by radicals with extremist views. Are they angry at not being in power? It appears that they are "rallying the troops" in readiness for a fight. Is this impending conflict, seeing those of the centre-right having to move further to the right, and away from the sensible centre that they once proudly occupied?

"Never look a gift horse in the mouth" we are told, as we are growing up. Great things can often happen when opportunities present themselves. Does this explain the "looting" that occurs, when law and order disappears during violent protests? Does our brain receive a surge of adrenaline, that sees some individuals, "recklessly" unable to stop themselves from breaking the law?

Indeed, just how much adrenaline surges through someone when they commit a serious felony? Conversely, which feel-good endorphin is released into the brain of those police officers or law-abiding citizens, that do good and make society a better place?

Whether it be right, wrong, left-leaning or right-leaning, we all have our differences and up until recently, have been able to harmoniously co-exist. We do however, have a predisposition to taking sides. Whilst we were growing up, our parents would always seek to resolve a sibling dispute amicably, through reasoning and by not taking sides. They gave us food, shelter, and the encouragement to grow and become independent. But today, how many people can say their parents, or teachers for that matter, gave them advice about political persuasion? Who is arbitrating on prevalent bias?

Another trait of humans is our desire to congregate together. "Safety in numbers" has always been considered a means of ensuring successful existence. Just as we have a flock of sheep or pod of whales, so too did we as humans, have our own groupings. Having things in common, saw us form tribes, gangs, teams, communities, and nations. It also gave rise to political parties, as we had a belief in the best way to achieve an outcome or govern a community.

As humans, probably the greatest endorphin release comes from being in "love." It makes us feel warm and fuzzy inside. To know that we are wanted and loved, is a powerful aphrodisiac. It is an addictive emotion and we crave it more and more. It can also send us crazy, make us do silly things, and unfortunately, also make us do bad things when it is taken away or removed.

Our individual feelings and actions can be influenced by adrenaline, endorphins, and even hormones! Likewise, allegiances we develop, occur through derived experience. The level of passion we exhibit for different things (or political parties), will vary according to the fulfilment and satisfaction we derive from desired outcomes.

"Petulance" is common in humans, when we don't get what we want. But we have learnt to "knuckle down" to the task at hand, and work harder to fulfil our dreams. Sometimes you have to "light your own fire." Today however, internal drive and fortitude is lacking in many and is in short supply. Our young seem content to blame others for their "lot in life," rather than go out and get it.

You only have to look at America, with its Trump Derangement Syndrome afflicting the Democrats and the media of the left. They didn't like the 2016 election result, and have set about removing Donald Trump by any means possible. They have resorted to corrupt and illegal tactics, and have set out to vilify anyone who is a supporter of the American President.

The "human psyche" also has an inherent desire to back the underdog. History taught us the outcome of the "David and Goliath" stoush. Think of a sporting contest between two teams or two individuals who you do not support or identify with. In the majority of cases people will tend to barrack for the "underdog." Is it just for the feel-good factor if the underdog wins? Or is it because they like to "go against the grain?" (defy conventional wisdom). Does this mentality in part, explain why socialism is so popular at present, given that the "have nots" are more disadvantaged than the "haves?" This would appear to help explain why there is growing fanaticism around social issues at present.

"Guilt" is a horrible experience for humans. It always leaves an uneasy feeling in your stomach, that something is not right. This unpleasant experience is chemically created through our adrenal glands. It helps to explain why equality and fairness are so sought after. The feel-good factor of encouraging redistribution of wealth through the social system, should not be underestimated.

"Denial" is also a common behaviour characteristic. Nobody wants to be blamed for someone else's misfortune. As such, we are all in a hurry to apportion blame for things that go wrong, on someone else. This can create a dismay towards others and when the misfortune is severe, it can lead to extreme hatred or "wrath." Within hatred, "anger" is lurking near the surface, ready to explode. This would certainly account for the venom in the hatred the socialists have for capitalism.

Bias or favouritism is rampant in society today. We view favourably, anything that serves our needs positively. If we are benefitting from something, we don't want that thing to change or be removed. So, we build up our self-defences to prevent that happening. We will do whatever it takes to maintain our goal or make our life better. It is human nature to try to attain what we need by any means (hunt), and then to protect what is acquired. (gather)

As in any contest, opponents will do what it takes to win. In the case of political parties, they aim to recruit (increase supporter base) in order to maintain their power or to attain power. With a limited voter base, the ability to attract voters has seen the left, pursue any policy whatsoever, that can attract those who have not been treated fairly or equitably. They have embraced wokeness. They have infiltrated media outlets, to deliver a biased version of all current events and affairs, so as to appear a viable voter choice.

There is one word that is perhaps synonymous with affairs today. "Sloth." A lack of vigour or even laziness towards action or activity. In its extreme, it can even refer to the denial of another's right to exist. Could this sin explain the rising levels of passion that are delineating the two sides of traditional politics. Despite a common life goal of health, wealth, and happiness, is "sloth" a reason why we haven't all embraced the need to save the planet from global warming? Or why we all haven't sought to work hard and better our lives? Or perhaps why the right, has not stood up to the vitriol of the left?

Looking at these different aspects of human anatomy and behaviour, you cannot help to notice that inherent are the "seven deadly sins." Pride, envy, gluttony, greed, lust, sloth, and wrath. As the church struggles for relevance today, the extent of these sins on widespread display, is like never before. And with record inequality dividing the population, this bears paying attention to.

History and the study of religion, has shown that the seven deadly sins are believed to "endanger one's salvation." The Catholic Church has used the concept of the seven deadly sins to curb the inclination towards evil. Are we once again seeing the rise of evil, and the seeds of war being sewn, in this conflict between the left and the right? Are these behavioural traits more prevalent now, due to the growing ignorance of the church and religion?

Is this the reason why Christianity is under the same attack as capitalism and Western civilisation? As the radical left have grown in strength, among their arsenal, is a willingness to deface or destroy churches, and to denounce anyone of Christian or Catholic faith. Why such hatred among the left?

Their obsession with equality, has seen the lefties now throw the accusation of "racist" towards anyone who stands in their way. It is as though if you have more wealth than someone, then somehow you are racist. Blatant disregard for the truth, and no respect for law and order, are the signs of a societal apocalypse. When are those from the right going to stand up to the mob, in order to restore peace and stability?

7.3 Behaviour

There is no doubt that some grow up less fortunate than others. Broken families can lead to a poor education, relatively poor wealth, and poor living standards. This can lead to juvenile delinquency and a troubled adult life. It is unfortunate for that minority, and it does impose a cost on Western nations as our policing, court, and jail systems seek to reform the miscreants.

This system of rehabilitation is not perfect, but it is societies' way of trying to remain inclusive for all. A law and order system to protect the law-abiding innocent from those that wish to do us harm is expensive, but is a major benefit derived from the wealth created by capitalism. And it must be preserved for society to remain civilised.

Policing is necessary to protect ordinary folk on the streets in their day to day activities. This also requires our law makers (elected officials, politicians and governments) to impose and regulate strict, fair, and understandable, rules and regulations. If they fail to exert strength through authority, the chain of command collapses and the system fails. "Fish rot from the head first." Senior government officials need the courage to set laws that appeal to the majority, rather than try to appease minority groups. In an evolving world, it is a never-ending battle to get the balance right.

Mandated laws if they go too far, can impinge on our liberty and start to create social unrest. Think everchanging road speed limits, mundane activities attracting penalties, cyber-crimes, social-distancing police, and the plethora of surveillance cameras on every street corner, and in every building. It is like the state has complete "control" over us, not unlike that envisaged by George Orwell, in his book "1984."

It is annoying to pay infringement notices issued in the mail, but at the end of the day, our government is only trying to protect us. It can make you angry at times, and make you want to rebel. Thankfully, we are taught that "if you do the crime, you do the time." We soon learn not to repeat our mistakes.

A "necessary evil" if you like. The same can be said of a strong military defence for a nation. A country that has to provide for its people, will be envious of a country rich in food and resources. No wonder China wants to "own" Australia. Trade occurs in peacetime, but in times of conflict, those with wealth, resources, and assets, are a prized target of the enemy. Defence spending by governments does detract from funds available to address other important issues, but it is vital for security, and to protect the population.

It is no coincidence, that the United State of America has the most powerful and feared military, to protect its enormous economy.

Hence the term super power. But it also has, as a consequence of this, a large inequality in the wealth of its people. Coupled with a large black indigenous population, and extensive migration from Latin America, it is now confronting a social revolution, where impatience at inequality is impacting law and order.

Australia and the United Kingdom too, are facing growing social unrest, borne out of frustration at rising living costs, and at government inaction to combat this. It appears though, that the arguments for action on these matters, are at the heart of the socialist culture wars. And any excuse will do. Racism, immigration, sexuality, culture, and religion, are all being used as an excuse to address perceived differences.

While right-leaning governments set policy to propel the economy to create wealth to address social issues, those of the left, are quickly becoming the face of the socialism revolution. Human minds and behaviour are being split in two. Rational behaviour by far too many people is "on the wane." Those of the left "cannot see, or do not want to listen," to the arguments against socialism.

In fact, it is doubtful that they truly know what they are striving for. Many socialists are "sheep following blindly." All the while, progressive politicians have taken their "eye off the ball," and have been swept aside in this uprising, as they chase votes by any means.

7.4 Conditioning

As we go about our daily lives, we are constantly being rewarded or punished, and we quickly learn to modify our behaviour accordingly. It is wise to learn from experience, and to rationalise all the actions we take and decisions we make. But are we still able to do this in an informed, objective manner? It used to be the case, but not anymore.

The media has been compromised. Objective news bulletins have been replaced by opinionated, subjective reporting. Depending on which source of news you are exposed to, you tend to receive a biased view of proceedings. CNN, The BBC, and the ABC are three major sources of information, but they are hopelessly biased towards the left. The same can be said of the press and some famous newspapers. "The New York Times," "The Washington Post," and in Australia, "The Sydney Morning Herald" and "The Guardian," all report the news with bias. They have a strong allegiance with those of the left political persuasion.

To combat this, each nation does try to balance the ledger, by having alternate newspapers or TV channels that report in an unbiased manner. But do all readers perceive the difference? Or are we just made aware of this by the political commentators of the day? Do we consciously listen to political commentary and question what we hear?

Are we the subject of propaganda, to coerce us into a certain way of thinking, thereby making us inclined to behave, think, and vote in a certain way? Absolutely damn right we are! If you are not taught the difference between left and right, or even if you couldn't care less about it, there is a battle on for your hearts and minds. And that is why socialism is on the rise and growing in popularity.

The first objective of marketing is to identify your market. Clever advertising is persuasive. Subliminal messaging can also slowly convert your way of thinking. Repetition aids memory. We are constantly bombarded with propaganda. Our "iPhones" are littered with clickbait. We look at, and play with, our mobile phones incessantly.

We are obsessed with having the latest news or trends at our fingertips. Pedestrians have died looking at their phones, instead of watching out for oncoming traffic. There is always a colourful array of catchy headlines, designed to grab our attention. But delve a little closer and there can be seen, a strong narrative hidden in the headlines. It favours the left in a massively disproportionate way. One needs to read every headline with an ounce of scepticism. Check the source, know the author or publisher's intent, and you will view the headline in a different manner.

Google, Facebook, Instagram, Snapchat, Tiktok, and Twitter, send information, opinions, and divisive propaganda, around the world in seconds. They are highly addictive, and have been targeted by political parties. Users subscribe to and develop a loyalty towards, each or all of them. Advertisers and those with an agenda know this. These mediums are then used to corrupt the minds of future voters. Do the users really know they are being played? Personally, I don't think so!

Is it trendy to support issues that you had no previous interest in? Recent protests around the world on climate change, indicate that peer-group pressure is influencing the behaviour of our younger generation. Thousands of protesters around the world also recently marched in unison, protesting at the death in police custody, of George Floyd in Minneapolis, America.

But were these numbers a reflection of concern at racial tension or did they represent a hatred for the ruling class? Or something else like inequality? And why did these riots turn violent, with heavy looting, vandalism, assaults, and over twenty people killed? 700 police officers injured in America alone. This wasn't a peaceful protest that the leftist media would have you believe.

Why did these protests morph into complete hatred for police forces around the world? "Defund the police" quickly became the catchcry. There is not one society around the world, that can exist without law and order. Who and what is driving so many people around the world to behave so irrationally? Whether it be on social, economic, climatic, humanitarian, racial or religious grounds, there is a concerted effort to exaggerate our differences. To create dissention. In this volatile atmosphere, the anarchists of the left are thriving, as they mingle freely with the peaceful protesters.

"Agitators" are gaining prominence, and distorting the true facts or versions of events. Police are hesitant to quell dissention because their actions can inflame tensions. Some police departments in lefty states, are even being ordered to stand down. With everyone carrying a "iPhone" with embedded camera technology, police actions are being scrutinised, recorded, and uploaded, for all the world to see. The radicals crave the attention and it spurs them on, in their ill-conceived revolution.

They antagonise and vilify anyone who does not accept their view of the world. Sound familiar to dictatorship or communism? There is a leftist narrative that has collectively consumed every relevant issue.

In short, they want control.

7.5 Control

Control is derived from power. Those exerting control or seeking power, are either trying to direct or influence people's behaviour, or trying to manipulate a course of events to attain a desired outcome. Does this "ring a bell," and alert you to the real agenda of the socialists?

From the time we are born, our parents exert control over us. In part to protect us, but also to educate us, and to indeed, make their own lives a little bit easier. We learn routine, and through trial and error, develop discipline. This forges in us, what behaviour is expected of us in order to take our place in society. We are also taught self-control to protect us from bad habits such as over-eating. Self-control is also used to curb aggression, which can lead to civil disobedience or law-breaking misdemeanours.

As we near the completion of our formative years (school years), we come under the control of our future employers, elected governments, and appointed officials. Law and order make for an organised, regulated society, designed to allow everyone to interact without incident.

Numerous examples of this exist. Road rules limit and constrict the way we drive. Licensing laws prohibit what we can do (work), and where we can go (pubs and clubs). Taxation laws exert pressure on what we can earn and what we can do with our money. Council and local laws even dictate where and how we live. Government regulatory authorities control our sewer, stormwater, building design, water consumption levels, and even the temperature of the hot water we use. Be under no illusion, we are under more control than you realise.

Recent world affairs, have seen an over-reach on the amount of control impacting the quality of our lives. The progressive lefties are now trying to control our movements, thoughts, actions, opinions, and even the way we vote. As with any socialist uprising, the first casualties are the truth, our freedom of speech, and the loss of liberty.

Teachers are exerting control over what we learn, by subjecting our students to their socialist view of the world. Look no further than the climate change hoax as proof of this. The LGBT movement is trying to control our sexual development and orientation. Socialist activists are seeking to denounce the church and its offerings.

Recent social unrest has been the result of culture wars, and the woke movement trying to disparage all views of the world, expressed by people of right political persuasion. Woke keyboard warriors are even trying to control consumer spending, by labelling us as "racist," if we don't conform to their radical socialist views on equality. They are exerting pressure on companies to rename any product who's "branding" may currently cause offense.

Many outspoken, vocal lefty activists, have often failed in their own educational challenges. They have also failed in their employment experiences and personal life choices. Given that, they are playing the victim, and they now want you to fail too! They seek to destroy the capitalism which has allowed so many to thrive.

They have infiltrated many media outlets to deliver their propaganda and "stir up" trouble. They tell you racism is rampant in society, when clearly it is not. They cannot control climate change, yet will push policies, that they say can determine temperature changes. Pure lunacy, that needs to be seen for what it is. A grab for power!

They seek to destabilize elected governments, in lieu of offering effective alternate policies. When this cannot be achieved, you can "bet your bottom dollar," that they will try to control the outcome of future election results. At this point in time, the lefties are revelling in the ineffectiveness of measures to combat their aggressive protests and cancel culture.

They "gloat" about their power, which rises with media exposure, even if they haven't been able to turn this into electoral success. Like Venezuela and CHAZ (Capitol Hill Autonomous Zone in Seattle), their uprising is usually fleeting and short-lived. There is no obvious solid foundation upon which to consolidate new found control. These social revolutions, draw their strength from getting the "unruly mobs" to do their dirty work. Remember too, that the mob also includes lefty scientists and media outlets. But they can't keep "the wool pulled over our eyes forever." Sooner or later, the truth reveals itself, allowing ordinary folk to see the radical lefties for what they are. Agitators seeking control.

Learn this, and you will know how you need to vote in the years to come. Which brings us to the Chinese Communist Party. They are the "ultimate control freaks." China today, is the living proof of what the socialist "utopia" looks like. Here, you have no control of your own destiny. This socialist mecca, offers you no freedom of speech or opinion, no right to protest, no independence, and not even the right to control your own family size. You are in effect "under the thumb." That is the left for you. Just ask the freedom-loving people of Hong Kong how much fun it is to be living under communist rule.

At the end of the day, if you control the minds of the population, you can set the narrative. Erase the past, control learning, and you are on the way to power and control of our individual and collective destiny. Control is everything.

7.6 Narcissism, the socialist mecca

Understand narcissism, and you can almost forgive the socialists for their behaviour. Did I say forgive? No! Rather, narcissism is an explanation for socialist behaviour, much of which is insane, and certainly unforgivable. By its very definition, narcissism refers to excessive interest and admiration of oneself, as you seek success and perfection. There are countless examples of people who have been in relationships with narcissists, only to see the relationships becoming tumultuous, before finally failing. Is it any wonder that socialism and narcissism go hand in hand?

The following points are indicative of narcissism, and are also inherent, in the socialist behaviour witnessed in society today. Consider narcissists and socialists simultaneously. They are both seeking superiority through a sense of entitlement. They possess an exaggerated need for attention, control, and perfection. They are always blaming others (conservatives) for their woes, and deflecting attention away from the real causes of their misery; Lack of "control" and "money."

Narcissists lack clear boundaries and believe that everything belongs to them (true socialism). They lack empathy, are rarely apologetic, remorseful or guilty, and they lack emotional reasoning. Check out the BLM movement for examples of this behaviour.

The narcissists project anxiety on others. The conservatives can readily attest to this, as they are attacked by wokeness. In reality, it is the narcissists who feel vulnerable and repressed. They fear rejection and have a strong desire to be heard and included. That certainly explains the derangement at election results. Finally, they have an inability to communicate and work as a team. In other words, they hate the fact they are not in charge. Hence their petulance, and lack of bipartisanship in the political arena.

It is as though, if you can negate narcissism, you can quell an uprising in socialism. And just how is that done? Well, it seems that many in the West, are already on the right track. Firstly, the narcissists are not as smart as they have fooled everyone into believing (see global warming hoax).

You have to be mindful of their true nature. Open your eyes to their abuse, and detach from them and their arguments. By knowing their true motives, you are in a better position to put yourself first. Do not react to their jabs. Narcissists and socialists thrive on reactions, so it is best that you step back from direct confrontation with them. Adverse reactions, only serve to embolden their behaviour and belief in their narrative. It certainly explains why the BLM protests died out, without direct confrontation with armed police forces. The socialists only ended up destroying their own property and neighbourhoods, along with a few statues. "Silly buggers!"

Rather than get anxious about socialists, narcissists, and volatile behaviour, it is best to just ignore them, and to know that you cannot change their behaviour. Let them think they are winning, and just sit back at the elections, and watch them implode with rage, when they do not have the success they anticipate. Remember too, that some of their behaviour is insane. They truly do, need to seek help from the medical profession. No need to idolise them, place them on a pedestal, or follow their mantra. The West has certainly been gentle and patient to date, in tolerating the deterioration in civil behaviour of the socialists. We now know what we are dealing with. "He who laughs last, laughs loudest."

7.7 Trust and respect

These two words, are at the forefront in today's battle lines. Regardless of your political persuasion, we all strive to live a happy and fruitful life as individuals. How successful you are, is dependent on your character, your motivation level, who you know, and a little bit of luck. The education qualifications you obtain, and the wealth you accumulate, are testimony to your upbringing. Strong parental guidance and input when we are young, obviously helps you stay "on the right side of the tracks."

Strong internal drive and self-motivation, will inevitably lead to success. Along the way, you will have to "cross many bridges as you get to them," but these only serve to make us stronger. "Trust" is the key to improved quality of life. If you can be trusted, people will follow you, and put their faith in you. From trust, "respect" is earnt. Western society is blessed to have so many trusted and successful members, who serve to protect their respective countries. Exceeding this, a chosen few, have been democratically elected, to govern us and preserve our sovereign interests.

Trust and respect can be seen most clearly in the disciplined, regimented armed forces around the world. Here, you put your life in that of your comrades, and he puts his life in your hands. The ultimate trust.

Imagine if you will, what it would feel like to stand and fight for Australia. Be in that armoured vehicle, heavily armed with other elite soldiers from a diverse background. How would you feel standing next to a Muslim or even lefty Australian soldier, knowing he had enough bullets in his gun chamber to kill you and all your comrades? Know too, that the radicals of his chosen religion have called that all Western white people, (infidels) must die. It takes a lot of trust to know that your fellow soldier will not turn his gun on you! Years ago, you wouldn't give this a second thought, but today…? In years to come, will soldiers of hard-left or hard-right persuasion, be willing or trusted to fight side-by-side to defend a nation?

Do you trust your fellow countryman to keep his gun pointed at the enemy? The elite training of our armed forces, implicitly requires complete faith in the chain of command. It is a shame there isn't more of this in mainstream society. But, if ordered civilization decays much further, how long before we start getting deaths by friendly fire or vigilante killings? The left is readily admitting now, that it stands against capitalism, its virtues, and even Christianity. Are we heading towards civil wars? Afterall, they have been fought in the past over ideologies.

I don't know about you, but I have nothing, but immense respect for all our armed forces. Same too, for our police, doctors, paramedics, nurses, and fire brigade members. We owe it to them and ourselves, to resolve our differences within society in a fair, democratic manner. Not via the current vilification, protests, and anarchy that are pervading our society.

Oh, that's right. Only one half of society is playing up. The radicalised lefties are "upsetting the applecart." Why? They are not in power! That's why! Nothing more, nothing less! Just typical petulant human behaviour, made worse by the "have nots" growing dangerously large in number, and becoming outspoken, through the lack of persecution of their misdemeanours.

The brave individuals of our army, navy, and air force, are at the end of the day, serving to put the nations interests first. We all owe them our existence, and need to get over the internal bickering that is plaguing our society. The left, in seeking to overthrow capitalism, are in fact, "throwing dirt in the face" of our serving members in the armed forces. Remember "that!" when you next head to the ballot box.

It is no secret, that the lucrative jobs with high-paid salaries, are traditionally filled with trustworthy people. Their exemplary behaviour, intelligence, confidentiality, experience, and academic qualifications (superior education), sees "the cream rise to the top." But, is this still the case today? The papers and media are quick to point out the corruption and dubious behaviour, of the rich and famous, and also many of our elected politicians.

Money (gluttony) has corrupted certain individuals, and seen them become obsessed with power? Society, has grown tired of politicians spruiking their pre-election policy promises, and then not delivering on them when in office. When the constituents lose faith in their elected leaders, respect "goes out the window." Is this phenomenon now readily on display, as the left and right are caught up in the battle to end all battles?

The same can be said of the media. When certain media streams can promote lies as the truth, what are the ramifications for society? Are the constant riots and protests, a sign that the Western capitalist system is being eroded? The media is now complicit in the lack of integrity being displayed by of many of our elected leaders.

Our leaders from both the left and right have to stand up and fight for the truth, obeyance of the law, and civilized order. The fact that the left seem intent on dismantling law and order, would suggest that the time has come, for those on the right to "stand and be counted." Afterall, unlike our fine brave young men from yesteryear, we are not being sent to fight in the trenches, or to risk our life against a foreign enemy.

But we do have to stand up and fight, for our freedom and our right to free speech. Today's enemy is in the classroom, office, workplace, living next door, printing the newspapers, monitoring Facebook, manipulating google, is on the television, or is a box on a ballot paper. We have to trust our elected leaders to fight for what we voted for. We have to support, respect, and defend, our constitution from attack within, just as much as we have to defend our borders, from an attack from abroad.

While on trust, given the way the world is heading, do we trust the individuals running the election centres? Do we trust each other to vote only once? Do we trust the vote counters to record accurately, the results? Do we trust the mailed-in voting ballot papers? Given the fight going on for power, how tempting is it to rig election results? Afterall, there are many corrupt governments in Third World nations, only in power because of fraudulent election results.

Recent election results in the "five eyes" nations have allowed capitalism to thrive. But with the desperation now on display from the lefties, do we now trust them to be able to govern us in the future, in the manner they had before? If they are to get into power, can we now trust them to not change the constitution? Can they be trusted not to rewrite legislation on the methods of voting in the future?

No weapons needed in this current battle. Just respect for each other, tolerance, and a willingness to listen to and understand, common sense. The fact that the lefties have been currently immune from arrest for breaking the law on occasions, is a scary scenario for society. If law-abiding behaviour is not re-established soon, the anarchist's revolution, will sweep all before them. Then, capitalism and the Western world as we know it, will be finished.

Which brings us to today. With the conflict between left and right, guess who "is waiting in the wings?" Our communist friends from China! Do we trust them? Do we trust our politicians to stand up to them and call out their communist behaviour? Do we trust the motives of Chinese immigrants?

As for the virus that China unleashed on the world from Wuhan, do we trust the Chinese Communist Party, when they say, "they did everything possible to prevent the virus spread?" Apparently keeping international airports open, did not cause the virus to spread around the world. So says the Chinese Communist Party. Do you trust the Chinese enough, to believe the international enquiry findings into the origins of the covid-19 virus? Do you trust the Chinese denials, when our government informs us of cyber-attacks on government institutions from a foreign state?

As for the Chinese migrants who supposedly integrate into multi-cultural Western society, do you trust their motives, when they horde all the baby formula, face masks, toilet paper, hand sanitizer, and personal protective equipment, and send it home to China? Trust when broken, can be hard, if not impossible, to mend. Just ask any person who has had their personal relationship with someone, ruined by infidelity. Why are the left not concerned about the communist threat on the Australian Doorstep?

When economies crash, and law and order cease to exist, society as we know it will be finished. We will be back to living in tribes. Can we be trusted to prevent this pending Armageddon? Are you doing your bit? Can we trust China not to invade Australia? After all, it hasn't taken them long to recolonise Hong Kong, after it became annexed from the British Commonwealth. Funny too, how this happened while the West was distracted by the covid-19 pandemic, a virus unleashed by the CCP actions. I don't know about you, but I "smell a rat!"

In Australia, given the Labor party dealings with communist China, can we trust our lefty politicians enough to know that China are not "in their pockets?" When you look at the current state of Victoria, you have to wonder why the lefty State Government has latched onto the Chinese purse strings. The "belt and road" initiative undertaken by the Dan Andrews State Labor government, is almost "bordering on treason," given the current state of world affairs.

Now more than ever, is the need to understand where Western nations stand. Do you value your freedom enough, to back the capitalist system that has given us the greatest living standards in the world? Or are you happy to go down the proven, futile, socialist path to ruin, thereby handing Australia over to China?

7.8 Rewriting history

"Winners are grinners, and losers can do as they please." It's a mantra that has been passed down through the ages. Sport has helped "make the world go round." It also serves to provide an example of how there is more to life than just winning. No shortage of success and failure in sport, but plenty of proof that there is always tomorrow. Learn from defeat and do it better next time.

It has provided a harmless theatre for combat, and is willingly cheered on by the masses. It has bought joy or despair to individuals, teams, communities, states, and even countries. But what happens on the field, always stays on the field. A wonderful example of how an ordered society can witness a contest, but then move on to the next challenge. If only politics could follow in the same vein.

They say "history is written by the winners." There is some truth in this. Ancient history, tells of the rise and fall of early civilisations. We have all heard of the "Roman Empire." The advances the Romans made in architecture, military organisation, service provision (roads, water aquifers), and developing an ordered society, still influence our lives today.

History also tells the tales of the vanquished, and the conquered. Look hard at the evidence, and you can see why some ideas and civilisations failed. For example, different models of motor vehicle are superseded, as technological advances permit added features or better performance. You only have to look at the model of "iPhone" in your hand, to see the speed of change.

The point being, that mistakes have been made and history has acknowledged them, just as it has recorded triumphs and notable feats. History helps to confirm progress and to steer society in the general right direction. Why would you want to erase it?

Advances in technology, have consigned much to the dustbin. It used to be the case, that the outdated were consigned to the history books. Yet history is being denigrated today. We are a throw-away society, and are impatient. Very few, seem to consider our historical past, as an important source of education for our future. Without it, our continued development will become constrained.

History has a habit of repeating itself; look at the rise and fall of many civilisations. Also, the cyclical nature of alternate left and right leaning governments, is testimony to wealth creation followed by wealth sharing, to address subsequent inequalities. It is wise to learn from this. To do so, requires continued accurate compilation and recording of current affairs, so that future generations learn from our mistakes. This is wise and again reflects a confident, ordered society, moving in the right direction.

In recent times, so much social unrest has created a phenomenon never seen before. Those of the left, are seemingly ashamed of our history. In protest at inequality around the world, they have taken to destroying or defacing, statues and monuments of historically significant or famous people. The anarchists are intent on erasing from history, all pioneers of yesteryear that created our modern society. It is as if they are in denial of what has been achieved, and the means by which this has occurred. A cancel culture has "reared its ugly head."

Any literature, records, famous movies, television programs, or copy of anything with even a hint of inequality, are being removed or destroyed. Copies of the famous "gone with the wind" movie are now banned, confiscated and destroyed, books are being removed from libraries, and copies on the internet deleted. The famous "Thomas the tank engine" animated kids TV series, has been removed from the airwaves and rewritten, because there was inequality between the number of male and female engines. It is ludicrous. This is blatant sexism according to those of the socialist left. Who cares?

Comedy sitcoms that have been famously replayed on television for over forty years, have been removed because those of the left do not like their content. "Love thy neighbour," "Fawlty Towers," and "Bless this House," all favourites from the seventies, have been withdrawn, as they were deemed offensive. Please!

"Humphrey B Bear" has been entertaining and educating our kids for years. This simple show of an actor dressed as a bear was removed because of the bear costume worn on the set. Apparently, a bear in a top hat, waistcoat, and bow tie is offensive because he didn't have any pants on. For years, no one seemed to mind or even notice. That is, until the woke brigade decided that this is offensive. Why do they get to rewrite the textbook on what is proper and improper? Is the left thinking they are morally superior?

Be it the explorers, the artists, our governing founders, or anyone they don't agree with, the socialists want their relevance destroyed. Their memory and heroic exploits erased. And at the time of writing, no one appears capable of stopping them. To stand up to them, regardless of whether you are a civilian, politician, or a paid police officer, is to draw condemnation from the left, to the point of physical attack.

The left is no longer concerned about dealing with the facts. Fact-check is a new phenomenon used in the media, to check the factual validity of what is being spoken by prominent members of society. Groups of fact-checkers quickly and anonymously, research what is said and cross-check this against known statistics. Any distortion of the truth, is quickly used against that person to ridicule their point of view.

Things are fine, as long as you support your argument with true, accurate information. But the left become enraged, the minute you turn around and fact-check what their socialist leaders say. And the problem for the left, is that they lie, distort the truth, or just end up blatantly ignoring the facts, just to satisfy their narrative. The fact-checkers themselves are often biased. So, you end up with the ridiculous scenario where, independent panels will soon need to "check the fact-checkers who check the facts." Society has grown sick and tired of seeing this pathetic wokeness.

It is poignant to remember the wise words of Abraham Lincoln, the sixteenth president of the United States of America. "You can fool some of the people all of the time, and all of the people some of the time, but you cannot fool all of the people all of the time."

It is frightening to see the left totally ignore the law. But do they really want equality? Are they the biggest hypocrites and the biggest racists of all? "Um…let me get back to you on that one!" Can they truly fight and defend what they stand for? Erase history, and you soon forget that socialism and revolutions are doomed to fail. Is that their only plan? To hope that no one will notice or remember?

Most importantly, are those of the left, capable of creating sufficient economic growth to maintain an ordered society in the socialist "utopia" they seek? Ask the people of Venezuela for an answer to that one.

History would suggest, their behaviour is nothing more than a lust for power. Pure greed. As recent election results in the "five eyes" nations showed, the left cannot succeed in their desire to rule, at the ballot box. As Abraham Lincoln also famously said, "the ballot is stronger than the bullet." So, the left in their derangement, now seek to defy and take by force. Subtle at first, but like any revolution, they seek to attract support by trying to win the moral victory. Their voice grows, as the size of their movement is "perceived" to be increasing.

But the quiet, respectable folk keep defeating them at the general elections. These battles are ongoing. From the day a new government is sworn in, it immediately begins its battle to seek re-election. The years quickly roll by, with little being done from a policy perspective, as the opposing parties get bogged down contesting all legislation. Frustration starts to rise, and social tensions escalate at the perceived inaction.

Are the recent election results, a reflection of superior intelligence, and recognition of what has worked in the past? It appears that the majority of society understands history, even if mistakes have been made in the past. Or is it a fear of anarchy and a loss of civility should the socialists prevail? It appears that our older folk, still remember the tough times, and do not want to see a repeat of them. But what of our youth? Are they being objectively educated on the pros and cons of each type of governance?

The answer to the last question is a big, fat "no!" It is becoming apparent, that mum and dad have a vital role to play, and they too need to be armed with the truth and political understanding. Take away history, and our children's ability to rationalise and form their own opinions is diminished. They are being conditioned to lean to the left.

The teaching fraternity has been weaponised. Given they are a part of a union, and suckling on the public teat, it is little wonder they lean to the left. Afterall, at the end of the day, "it is every man for himself." Protect the payer and the payee will get to fight another day.

University, was supposed to be the last bastion of critical free thinking. But no, the march of the left through the institutions, has been going on now for some time. Rather than receive objective higher education, our young are subjected to the same leftist view of society. A significant number of senior academics, have never entered the real world, and are happy to exercise their power on campus, preaching the ways of the socialist progressives. Politics is rife on campus, as is the radicalisation of our youth. A quality higher education has "gone out the window," it seems.

Other graduates, wind up working in companies where they slowly instil their woke ways into the company work ethic. Soon some of these companies are so riddled with leftist ideology, that as a right-leaning voter, you won't last in this work environment. Scary, but true.

Times have changed. Today, you are advised to not even write your age on a job application, as you will be overlooked based on "ageism." Where does it end? We can't exist for long, if we all "bury our head in the sand," and pretend this crap isn't going on.

Companies in the woke world, are being shamed into employing future workers, according to gender quotas and racial diversity ideology. That's right, your qualifications become irrelevant, compared to the need to diversify and promote equality. Currently, there are many organisations reshuffling their director composition, to include more women on their boards. Talented males are also being overlooked, to ensure females are promoted to positions in upper management.

Once again, the "best man for the job" is being disregarded. It is little wonder, that business bankruptcy levels are at record numbers. Afterall, this is a means of destroying capitalism from within. Definitely time to "return the favour," when it comes to voicing your political opinions. If you don't want things to be this way, then you know what you have to do. At the very least, you need to make your vote count.

This urge to erase the past, is driven by the misinformed, and those who have failed in life. The non-contributors to society, are stuck in a time warp, created by leftist ideology. If you wish to have your future dictated by oppressors, then that "is a recipe for disaster." Without history, you have no future.

7.9 The decline of religion

There is little doubt that in recent years, the growing unrest in the West, has coincided with the decline of religion in society. Since the second World War, the liberated West has thrived on capitalism. Christianity was at the forefront of an ordered society. Judeo-Christianity underpinned the classical liberal view; that all people should be treated equally.

However, as the world became globalised, the movement of people, the spread of ideologies, and freedom of speech, saw a dilution of the common conventional wisdom. In the 1911 Australian Census, 96% of Australians reported themselves as Christian. By 2016, this number was down to 52 %, and a further one third, reported no religious belief at all. Multiculturalism, also saw the introduction of many different nationalities, who each had their own religious beliefs.

Reading of the bible and the new testament diminished. These scriptures were the founding document of Western culture. Respect and understanding of humanity, were intertwined in these readings, but with the decline of religion, the historical significance of our foundation is being lost. Our youth especially, are losing their sense of faith, and an understanding of the principles of our society.

The Catholic church, has also in recent times, been plagued with its own controversies. Catholic priests, have been the subject of abuse claims, including the "paedophilia of young altar boys." The lefty woke brigade, have taken to supporting any person who claims they were "abused" in the decades prior. This has weakened the "righteous image" of the church. Another ploy to bring down capitalism? Another trojan horse perhaps?

The LGBT movement, in their legalising of gay marriage, also divided the religious fraternity. Many pastors refused to marry same-sex couples, under the proviso that it was against the preaching of the bible. Other religious groups, such as the Muslims for example, do not recognise homophobia. Society is being divided.

Overseas, various religious groups are often at war with one another. Under the guise of religion, there have been battles for territory, the right to govern, and to manage differing ethnicities. This has clearly resulted in some people viewing religion indifferently, and with disgust in some cases.

The whole speed of life, and rising costs of living, have made it more difficult for parents to encourage their young to attend church. Parents are too time-poor, to spend a Sunday morning at church, like they had in their own younger days. The church used to be, one of the few things to be open on a Sunday morning. Today, weekend sport, twenty-four-hour shopping, electronic devices, and lucrative penalty rates for workers, have given rise to other alternatives for the population.

So, as our society turns its back on religion, while it is a personal choice, it is seeing Christianity on the wane in the West. The traditional belief that we are a common humanity, is being supplanted by identity politics, that is dividing us into tribes. These divisions, and rapidly rising inequality, are creating further social unease and giving rise to conflict.

You can rest assured, that recent world protests to remove any statue or monument, which may offend on the basis of perceived inequality, will soon result in attacks on religious buildings or monuments. Sure enough, as I write, there has been a spate of arson attacks on famous churches throughout Europe. Oh, so predictable. Again, the lefty brigade is seeking to destabilise.

To create their "utopia," they have to remove all understanding and proof, of the known conventional wisdom. Religion has been instrumental in our history and development. As George Orwell wrote, "the past was erased, the erasure was forgotten, the lie became the truth." The decline of religion, is having a massive bearing on local and international stability.

7.10 Devaluing science

Science has always been at the forefront of societal development. It has shaped our lives, helped us increase food production, taught us to fluoridate our drinking water, given us better hygiene, helped us live longer, and even given us a better means to defend ourselves. We have acquired knowledge, through observation and experiments into "cause and effect." In dealing with a body of facts or truths, we have learnt to systematically arrange and determine, what is best for us. Very smart. This is now under threat at present, due to the left socialist forces that are shaping our societies.

Scientists approach the unknown with objectivity, seeking conclusive outcomes. Through their research, they are able to formulate the best options and opinions; to advise leading governments and decision makers. At least, that is how it is supposed to work in theory.

Scientists are remunerated to prove theories and seek answers. Get a result, and they are quickly out of a job. Once we find a cure for cancer, there will be a lot of people out of work. And so, the merry go round continues. "We need to be paid a little bit more, just to be sure, and to confirm previous findings" is their mantra. "Money is the root of all evil!" Again!

Being human, scientists are also susceptible to bias, and can have pre-conceived ideas. They have the ability and capacity to identify, verify, validate, deny, falsify, misconstrue, corrupt, and deceive. In recent times, they have been at the forefront, of perhaps the greatest fraud perpetrated on mankind in history. The "global warming hoax," and the controversy, it subsequently "unleashed." This has quickly become the "trojan horse" of our time. More on that baby to follow.

Some scientific fields of discipline, have become shrouded in mystery and secrecy, others riddled with corruption, and others still, politicised by nations and political parties with different agendas. Look no further, than research into biological weapons of mass destruction. This has created an air of suspicion and scepticism, which is clouding the decision-making of leading political parties.

Governments turned to the scientific experts in 2020, as the world faced the covid-19 global pandemic. This has been an unmitigated disaster, with confusion, over-reaction, exaggeration of the consequences, lack of consensus, debate over treatment, and suspicion over its origins. All the while, government leaders stood by "impotently," as their economies crumbled, seemingly unable to be advised accurately by the scientists. People grew impatient at the inconsistent messaging from leaders, and frustrated at the differing levels of monetary support, offered to some sections of the community.

Scientists have made a lot of people bankrupt, unemployed, and destitute. Should we continue to naively, listen to the experts in our time of need? How the world's economies recover, remains to be seen. A "once in a life-time" event, has been handled relatively well by some of our leaders. It seems that their decision to close borders, has done more to preserve life and prevent further spread of the disease, than anything the scientific experts have offered.

The covid-19 virus only served to "throw fuel onto the fire" of inequality, and the dissension that was already permeating society. Clearly, society was not "all in this together." Public servants remained in paid employment, while the private sector was effectively shut down. "Social distancing" advised by the scientists, was not practised uniformly. Another source of growing dissension in society!

Even during worldwide lockdowns, the socialists took to the streets. It seems that those of the left, were allowed to conduct mass rallies, protesting at racial discrimination. Hundreds of thousands attended these rallies around the world. Many turned violent, with looting, assaults, vandalism, torching of vehicles and shops, and the desecration of government buildings, churches and monuments.

Meanwhile, a father and his son were not able to go fishing in Melbourne, during the lockdown. A dangerous precedent of "duality in standards" here. The socialist left, who want equality so much, were the most hypocritical of all, in defying the law.

The scientists haven't found a cure for the virus, they argue about the means of transmission, the incubation time, and even the origins of the virus. Scientists and doctors in Wuhan (China), even disappeared completely, depending on what they knew or tried to reveal. Clearly, the agenda of the Chinese Government, was more important in this case, than the safety and wellbeing of the local and international community.

Inconsistency in scientific information on the virus, is clouding the ability of the economy to recover. Our leaders, had listened to the scientific experts who got things terribly wrong. There is a lesson here. Should we also believe what the scientists tell us about global warming and climate change? It seems that a lot of science has been devalued and corrupted, to fit the socialist narrative of the left.

Scientific evidence can contribute to our understanding of social issues, but that doesn't take away from the need for public discussion, about the values that are going to be prioritised. For example, individual freedom, versus the common good. Nowhere is this more evident, than when looking at the "three trojan horses" of the socialist left.

8

The Three Trojan Horses

8.1 Which straw will break the camel's back?

Never, has there been three forces to hit the world simultaneously, with such ferocity. A "perfect storm" if you like. As a leading Western nation, Australia is most fortunate to have a stable system of government, and relatively low national debt by world standards. That said, our existence in this global village, has been recently rammed home to us. Despite our geographic isolation, we have endured precisely, what the rest of the world is going through, and simultaneously!

What we are witnessing play out on television overseas, is mimicked here, almost straight away. It is unprecedented in its intrusiveness, with seemingly no end in sight. Our leaders at present, are reluctant and hesitant to confront the issues, for fear of further alienating different sections of society. The Australian Liberal government is seemingly, on the verge of bowing to many demands of the left. This is despite the mandate we gave our right-leaning elected government. You could say regrettably, that the socialists are getting their way.

Previous chapters have highlighted political differences, and traditional causes, but what are the antagonists which expedited this dangerous shift to socialism. The first of these is the "trojan horse" of our times, affectionately referred to by the left, as "global warming." This battle has been compounded, with the covid-19 global pandemic currently gripping the world. Finally, when we are all "at our wit's end," along comes the George Floyd killing, which has seemingly tipped the world over the edge.

There is that dangerous old adage. "When you have got nothing, you have got nothing to lose." Is this phenomenon driving the reckless, selfish behaviour of the progressive socialists?

8.2 The global warming hoax

Spurred on by the extremist views of the "Greens," worldwide concern for the ongoing stability of the planet, was made the number one issue for the United Nations to address. A plethora of scientists put forward theories and data, to suggest that the earth's core temperature was rising, and that this would have catastrophic results for humanity in years to come.

In 2016, the United Nations Framework Convention on Climate Change (UNFCCC), put forward a framework (Paris Agreement) for greenhouse gas reductions; through adaption, mitigation, and reporting of performance. The countries of the world agreed to reduce their individual carbon emissions, for the betterment of mankind as a whole. It was perceived that rising levels of carbon dioxide, were responsible for global warming. Chlorofluorocarbons (CFC's) were burning a hole in our "ozone layer," which has protected us from the harshness of the sun's rays.

Scientists told us that this was going to melt the polar ice caps, creating massive rises in sea-level, thereby inundating low-lying regions and countries. This would displace millions of people worldwide. We were also told that extreme weather events such as hurricanes and cyclones, would become more frequent, extreme, and lead to the costly destruction of property, and the death of many.

Global warming is dangerous, the lefty scientists tell us. The planet will warm by one or two degrees over the next 50 years, they say. Disastrous for humanity they preach. Yet, everyone I know, cannot wait to take a holiday in the tropics or somewhere much warmer. Thirty degrees centigrade, is much more appealing than the zero-twenty degrees centigrade temperatures, on offer in places where half of the populace resides. Just a little bit "hypocritical," to say that a warming planet will be bad for us.

And here is where the wedge being driven into society, began to divide us. While some scientists were urging governments to act quickly, there were other scientists, who could not provide any empirical evidence to back up the projections.

Greek mythology tells of the Greek battle to defeat the Trojans, and take control of the city of Troy. After ten years of trying, the Greeks appeared to concede to their rivals. They constructed a massive wooden horse, rolled it up to the gates of the city of Troy, but then walked away, and sailed off into the sunset. The Trojans, thinking this was a victory gift, then rolled the horse into their town. Unknowingly, a selected armed force led by Odysseus, were concealed inside. They emerged from inside the horse, and combined with other Greek forces who sailed back during the night, fought and defeated the Trojans.

A classic example of a trick or strategy, used to dupe and defeat the enemy. Which brings us to the global warming hoax. A massive hoax perpetrated by the left, to "redistribute wealth throughout the world." Close down our largest industries of coal and mineral extraction, and instead, open up whole new industries in renewable energy provision. I wonder how many lefties and socialists have shares in companies, which will supply the products necessary for renewable energy creation? Malcolm?

There is little doubt, the climate is changing. It always has and it always will, but certainly not to the extent that the socialists and Greens are proclaiming. Any scientists who disprove this theory are quickly shouted down, ridiculed, or even fired from their place of work. "Climate deniers" is the taunt and accusation levelled at them. But what of the facts?

There is significant empirical evidence, to suggest that sea-levels are not rising at all. "Scare-mongering" news reports showed that a couple of low-lying South Pacific islands and atolls, were being inundated by rises in sea level. However, aside from tidal fluctuations, water finds its own level, so it cannot be rising in one location and not somewhere else. Liquefaction is a well-known process, where porous land masses allow groundwater to rise as the soil particles settle, especially when subjected to movement or force.

It was this process causing these atolls to sink, which was deliberately ignored, in order to fit the narrative; of global warming and rising sea levels. This region, where these "sinking" atolls were documented, is in "the ring of fire." A part of the planet "notoriously" subjected to extensive tectonic activity. It is a scientific fact, that some land masses are lowered, due to movement of the earth's crust (subduction). This itself, would give the alternate image of a "rise in sea level." Easy to dupe people this way.

Another point to make on sea level changes. The only way for them to rise, is for ice sitting over land masses, to melt and slide into the sea. And that is going to take a lot more than one or two degrees in temperature change. The modelling put forward by Al Gore in "An Inconvenient Truth," was "sensationalism" in all its "biased glory." His graphs showing predicted sea level rises, ignore one important fact.

Water expands as it freezes. As such, if the polar caps were to start melting, the first thing to happen, would be a drop in sea-level. Don't believe me? Put a plastic bottle of water into the freezer, and then see if it remains in shape when it solidifies. Oh dear! The lefty scientists won't tell you that! But then again, they are hiding on university campuses, apparently lacking experience in the real world. "People in glass houses should not throw stones!"

Certain institutions (e.g. Bureau of Meteorology), have set about rewriting the recorded facts and figures, to back up these ridiculous claims and predictions. Government agencies have recently been caught "homogenizing" historical temperature records. This involved deleting previously-recorded maximum temperatures, and inserting lower temperature figures. When these figures were extrapolated onto graphs with todays' recorded temperatures, this gives the appearance of a trend of rising temperatures.

When questioned about these actions, meteorology and agency officials suggest they do this because temperatures recorded many years ago were perceived to be inaccurate. If that is the case, why are all temperatures re-recorded as having been lower and not higher? Just like the Trojans, it appears we are being conned. Conniving buggers!

Indeed, today there are countless examples of temperature recording stations, exhibiting their lowest temperatures ever recorded. Scientists (that are not corrupt) even suggest that the ozone holes, over the poles, have disappeared. Also, rather than retreating polar caps, there is evidence to suggest, that the size of the polar caps is actually increasing. That the earth may actually be cooling. But these theories are ridiculed and shouted down, as they destroy the integrity of the leftist argument. Scientists who question the validity of the global warming data are disappearing just like our statues. Sound familiar? Indoctrination springs to mind.

Of note here, is the fact that the earth is uniquely blessed in its orbital distance from the sun. We are fortunate that we are not too close to burn up, and yet not too distant from the sun to freeze to death. Consider the fact that in our present orbit, on the earth's surface, it is a mere 6,400 kilometres or so from the equator, to either the frozen north or south pole. It follows that if our orbit was a further 6,400 away from the sun, there is a likelihood, that a whole lot more of our planet would be frozen over. Also, a slight variance in our elliptical orbit of the sun, could be the cause of changes in global temperatures, and not man-made activity as the left would have you believe. Anyone got a tape measure?

Our planet is also susceptible to fluctuations in temperature, due to solar flares. We orbit a sun which itself, is an unstable evolving mass. Volatility on the sun's surface, can cause radiating heat emitted to fluctuate in intensity. This phenomenon can also wreak havoc on the earth's recorded temperatures. Again, the lefties conveniently manipulate these statistical anomalies, to support their narrative.

Variations is recorded temperatures, can also occur due to volcanic activity here on earth. Major volcanic eruptions such as Mount St Helens (1980), and Mount Pinatubo (1991), emitted enormous amounts of volcanic ash into the atmosphere. This can have a bearing on the short-term temperatures worldwide, as the ash enters the stratosphere and insulates the earth, warming and then cooling the earth by a few degrees. Again, this point is disregarded, by those making an argument to support the left. They continually overlook these facts, in their blind pursuit of the socialist narrative.

Climate scepticism is thankfully on the rise, as people begin to question the validity of the preposterous claims from the left. With the advent of new information, and recognition of these facts invalidating the extent of global warming, the socialist left has resorted to a new tactic. As the extent of this hoax becomes apparent to those without bias, the left now fondly refers to global warming as "climate change." They have been caught out, with some scientists even back-tracking, on their early claims about global warming.

As an example, it was claimed that global warming was destroying the Great Barrier Reef (north eastern Australia). However recent research is indicating that the reef is steadily growing. Cyclical changes in the reef appearance were previously being used to validate the global warming statistical evidence. Nobody, it seems, bothered to ask the tourism operators about the stability and health of the reef. How convenient.

Any significant weather event, is quickly seized upon as evidence of the lefty predictions. Bushfires, cyclones, flash floods, droughts, and hurricanes, have become tools used to push the left narrative. Evidence that we have to act quickly. The only way to eradicate these events, is to adopt green policies, endorsed through the Paris Agreement. "Supposedly!"

Despite a multitude of social and economic issues confronting respective societies, every general election is now being contested primarily, on green issues such as climate change. This cultural battle has given strength and voice, to the socialist left. It is almost as if, they think they have the power to alter and control the weather.

The leftist media join in this scare-mongering, by exaggerating the magnitude, cost, and even death tolls, of significant weather events, all to support their argument. They sensationalise everything, to condition us on the need to act. The Australian bushfires of 2020, were reported as the "worst of all time," in terms of fatalities, destruction of property, and total area of land destroyed or burnt. But, a quick check of historical records, reveals that fires of greater magnitude, have been happening for decades. The "fact-checkers," mysteriously disappeared.

Indeed, there is a strong correlation between Australia's recorded bushfires, and the cyclical influence of the El Nino and La Nina weather phenomena, which are driven by ocean currents. Australia was poetically, "a land of droughts and flooding rains" according to Dorathea Mackellar, long before global warming and climate change were even thought of. But this is once again, conveniently overlooked by the left and their media accomplices.

The severity of the Australian fires, was actually due to tremendous fuel loads present in fire-prone regions. Fire requires oxygen, fuel, and a source of ignition for it to occur. Oxygen is in abundance and naturally occurring. Ignition cannot be prevented due to lightning strikes, sparks from electrical short circuits in powerlines, and unfortunately, spates of arson by pyromaniacs. But the fuel loads of debris on the ground, were the direct result of green and lefty activism, that sought to ban the backburning which reduces future fuel load hazards.

Common sense warnings, by concerned locals in fire-prone regions, about the dangerous build-up in fuel load, were repeatedly ignored, by lefty and green local government officials. Yet the left, is quick to apportion blame for the bushfires, to their global warming narrative. Totally wrong, and yet given plenty of airtime, by their lefty media buddies. Is this another deliberate attempt to destabilize, and destroy capitalism, by stealth?

There was significant destruction of property during these fires as well. Urban expansion has seen the development of residential areas encroach on natural bushland. It is this population growth factor which is contributing to the "loss of property" numbers, as more people build in fire-prone regions. But no, the lefties will have you believe, that the destroyed property numbers are because of global warming. The brainwashing is enough to make you angry! Or write a book!

In fact, the media were so quick to "catastrophize" the series of fires, the rest of the world could be forgiven, for thinking that the whole of Australia was on fire. Such was their exaggeration of the extent of the fires. Those on the right knew the real cause of the fires, but their calls were drowned out by the climate activists.

Right-leaning governments, being more conservative, were also questioning the enormous costs of meeting Paris Agreement targets. Coal mining has always provided industrialised nations, with a cheap and reliable source of electricity. However, it has a high carbon footprint (excessive carbon emissions). The only known way to reduce the national carbon footprint, is for the introduction of renewable sources of energy, to replace the burning of coal.

People, states, and countries, were quickly divided on the issue. Those of the left, in their progressive ways, were adamant in their desire, to convert to wind and solar energy, in order to power the electricity grid. They seem unconcerned at the mammoth costs, associated with replacing coal-fired power plants, with wind turbines and solar panels. Nor were they concerned by the fact that Australia's enormous financial sacrifice, would only reduce world temperatures by 0.1 percent at best. Even that figure, would require every other nation to simultaneously achieve their targets.

Common sense will tell you that a country of twenty-five million, cannot do the "heavy lifting" for a world inhabited by nearly eight billion people. Have our leaders "lost their marbles?"

Despite abiding by Paris Agreement targets, Australia is yet to embark, on the serious nation-changing path down the renewable's road. Those of the right have simply pointed out that "the wind doesn't always blow, and the sun doesn't always shine." The lefties are conveniently content to ignore this fact.

Electricity, also needs to be affordable and reliable, and so the electricity grid would need reliable backup power. Neither side of the political spectrum, can agree on how to do this in a cost-efficient manner. The 2019 Australian general election was contested primarily on this issue. The Green/left coalition lost an unlosable election over the matter. Clearly "jobs and growth" were more important to the people. It is economic suicide to attempt to adopt green renewable-energy policy, and currently, there is debate as to what percentage of electricity should even come from renewables.

Even "dyed in the wool" leftist supporters, know the massive costs of renewable energy, and yet they blindly push ahead with their plans. Even though they lose at the ballot box, they are determined to have their way. But what has been highlighted, once again, is their massive hypocrisy.

They do not acknowledge the massive carbon footprint that their "green new deal" plans will leave. The construction of the massive wind turbine blades, the costly solar panels, and the extravagant backup batteries, all require massive burning of fossil fuels (coal) during their manufacture. When they are confronted about this, they "disappear quicker, than a virgin on prom night" or they change the subject altogether. Clearly, no thought has gone into their plans.

Piers Akerman (Daily Telegraph, 2020), said it best when he stated "in the trashed world of woke protests, the truth stands for nothing. The vehement argument for action on climate change, loses its lustre, when the conservatives (those of the right) use their prudent economic mastery, to validate the costs of these actions. This then sees the left hijack, any other cultural issue that will distract from the facts, and also subvert followers of other issues, to take up their cause."

In other words, those of the left are quick to jump on any cultural difference that builds a momentum against those of the right. In recent times the animosity is bordering on hatred. It is tearing Western nations apart. But late 2019, saw a whole new faceless enemy, distract and isolate, the nations of the world.

8.3 Covid-19, the great leveller

Late 2019, saw the emergence of sketchy reports, about some unknown illness emanating out of Wuhan, the capital city of the Hubei Province in the Peoples Republic of China. In a city of over eleven million people, doctors in local hospitals were reporting a highly infectious virus, that was quickly spreading and resulting in mass casualties. Doctors notified local authorities, and a few even went as far as to spread the word to overseas colleagues via email, seeking answers as to what it may be.

Later identified as "covid-19" (corona virus December 2019), this virus was similar to the swine flu and SARS, which had both preceded it, in that it was another Severe Acute Respiratory Syndrome. A highly contagious virus, which resulted in death to many who contract it, and with no known treatment. That much was known, but thereafter, this illness has been shrouded in mystery, secrecy, and controversy. What has followed, has taken the world to a whole new level of unrest, anxiety, and distrust.

At first, The Chinese Communist Party (CCP) thought they could contain it. They isolated buildings and hospitals where there were reported cases. Fearing an uncontained spread, they then locked down the city of Wuhan, and closed down all domestic air travel. They also embarked on silencing all initial responders and reporters of this virus. I wonder why that might be?

Doctors who tried to alert the Western world and The World Health Organisation (WHO), quickly disappeared and along with them, any emails concerning their efforts to raise this fact. Foreign reporters were expelled from the region, and there was a veil of secrecy in place around the whole of China. The rest of the world acted unconcerned at the looming story, thinking they had seen these outbreaks play out in the communist land before.

Interestingly though, Wuhan houses a high security, Infectious Diseases Laboratory, which was conducting secretive research on bat viruses at the time. This venue too, was locked down by the CCP, as officials prevented any foreign inspection of the premises. The Chinese even resorted to accusing the United States of inserting the Virus into the local Wuhan population.

Others believe that Chinese wet markets (which trade in an assortment of live animals kept in squalid, unhygienic conditions), were the likely source, although researchers of virus vaccines have since dismissed this theory. Most suspect that the virus was "inadvertently" released from the laboratory, and into the local community near the wet markets. Afterall, it wouldn't be the first time a virus was unleashed upon the world, from this region.

This theory is best supported by the actions of the CCP authorities themselves. This is where things have got murky for the rest of the world. The CCP closed down its own domestic air travel, but allowed international flights to continue for another six days. Was this intentional, to let the virus spread around the rest of the world, carried unknowingly by those departing China? Some believe this to be the case. Indeed, China was in the middle of a trade war with The United States of America at the time.

President Donald Trump, in his Pro-America way, was improving the terms of trade for American interests. These initiatives were starting to have an adverse impact on the Chinese local economy. In coercing the Chinese to accept revised terms of trade, America had regained the economic ascendancy between these two competing economic super powers. However, the CCP, in its arrogant and conniving way, had inserted a tiny clause into the agreements, which stipulated that deals could be cancelled or re-evaluated in the event of an "unforeseen act of nature." How convenient!

Was this virus, a deliberate means to undo the agreements that had been recently been signed? Whether or not this is the case, the virus was to quickly change the course of nature, and inflict upon the world, the greatest economic recession of all time.

The CCP had previously advised the WHO, that the virus was contained, and in any case, it could not be transmitted human to human. Why did they lie about this? Meanwhile, people started dying in large numbers from the virus in Italy, and this became the world's first new "hotspot" for the disease. The Italians had, in the years prior, welcomed a large Chinese migrant population, as the Chinese proved to be a cheap source of labour for their farming regions. Hence the logical spread of the virus there.

Italy is also popular with tourists, and it didn't take long, for the virus to spread to other regions throughout Europe. At this point, the WHO did nothing to address this issue, other than to advise not to speculate on the origins or nature of the disease. It merely reiterated what it had been told by the CCP. Was the WHO, corruptly beholden to the CCP? Was the WHO reluctance to declare a pandemic, out of fear of retribution from the Chinese?

The world got angry at the inaction of this organisation, as it merely advised not to stigmatise or denigrate the Chinese, who were busy covering up the virus origins. A typically woke stance, where inequality and divisions were not to be encouraged. But this stance was deemed too weak and ineffectual. The WHO was now impotent! I was going to say like "a ship without a rudder," but that is far from the case. It now appears most likely to be under the stewardship of the CCP.

So much so, that America under Trump, has withdrawn from funding the organisation in the future. Australia also led the world in calling for an independent enquiry into the outbreak of the virus, which has only served to inflame tensions with the CCP. There are now heightened tensions between the East and the West, which are "applying the blowtorch" to current trade wars.

Shocked at the rapid spread of the virus by air-borne means, countries around the world closed their borders, and shut down international air travel. But it was a case of "too little, too late," as the virus had already been carried around the world. The "window of opportunity" to have done this successfully, had been effectively "slammed shut" by the CCP, who allowed international travel for a further six days after they had shut down their own domestic air travel.

The world wants to know why this suspicious behaviour occurred. What were the "true CCP motives" of this action? Were they hoping for a pandemic to slow Western economies, so as to give themselves further economic strength? Many experts also consider this behaviour to be an "act of war."

Further, the virus was now rampant on cruise ships that were carrying passengers around the world. At the time of writing, there are some 42,000 workers stranded on cruise liners around the world, unable to disembark, due to the virus being prevalent on board their ships. The lockdowns were effectively, a "catalyst" to shut down the world's economies. A financial storm of unprecedented magnitude, was about to engulf the world for the first time, and pose the greatest threat to the modern economy, since the GFC in 2008.

Unemployment began to rise rapidly as people lost their jobs, especially in the airline, hospitality and tourism sectors. Anger, dismay and suspicion, grew at the Chinese who were responsible, although they repeatedly deny culpability. Other nations noted that, while they themselves were subject to rising infection and mortality rates, Beijing was remaining virus free. How was this possible? Were the reported CCP statistics believable? Why did millions of Chinese "iPhone" accounts, suddenly show no further calls being made, shortly after the virus outbreak? Why did satellite images of Wuhan hospital carparks, show traffic chaos in and around them, in the months before the supposedly-reported, virus outbreak date?

Unfortunately, infection rates begun to rise locally in Australia too, despite closed borders. Federal and State Governments were forced to initiate "draconian social distancing measures." These consisted of the closing down of all schools, sporting events, and public gatherings. Shops, pubs, gyms, clubs, and even work places, were placed into lockdown.

Fearing an economic meltdown, governments were then forced into emergency stimulus spending, to compensate those who had lost their employment. It should be noted, that they also did this cynically, to prevent sharp rises in unemployment, which is seen as a gauge of their economic performance. Clearly, "perception is everything," and so the governments knew that their handling of these affairs will be remembered at election time.

In reality, this was a means to buy time to prevent the inundation of our limited health facilities by infected patients, and to also buy time in the race for the development of a vaccine against the virus. But it was ruining economies like never before. The share market collapsed, GDP levels contracted sharply, and even the banks intervened, to suspend or defer mortgage repayments for home loan customers. The shutdown could not go on unabated into the foreseeable future. Society would soon collapse, without the government driving initiatives to reboot the economy.

Funny though, how "another group" didn't seem to mind all this. While there was widespread grief at our health and financial predicament, there was "palpable joy" by many on the left. Never had capitalism been decimated and dismantled so quickly. And never had so much public spending occurred so quickly, and without debate.

Clearly, the spoils of capitalism had given the Australian government, a financial "treasure chest" with which to finance its emergency stimulus packages. But the socialist left went very quiet on the government stimulus spending. The "call quickly went out" to keep these measures in place longer than originally intended, and with no regard to the consequences, nor the amount of national debt being accrued.

In Australia, this accruing national debt, took away the impetus from a Liberal government, that was on target to deliver a budget surplus. (Surpluses are needed to pay down previous debts). So, in essence, the stimulus only served to compound current economic woes.

After three months of containment measures, infection rates and mortality numbers began to drop, as transmission of the virus diminished, and lockdown measures appeared to have been successful. It was time to open up the economies, to restore financial stability, and to begin repaying the accumulated government and private debts.

Once again, the left was controversial to say the least, in their response to these re-opening measures. In Australia and throughout other regions in the world, it appeared that regions under leftist control had a different agenda. Regions governed locally by leftist councillors, were keeping their local areas locked down longer, while the rest of society opened back up for business. We were told "we are all in this together" but this was clearly not the case.

Likewise, workers from the public sector, were treated differently to those employed in the private sector. During the pandemic closures, public workers were given full pay or even pay rises, whilst many in the private sector, had to close for all but essential work. Again, this has been dividing society.

Regions under leftist control, were also subjected to different health instructions and guidelines. Here, the population was required to wear a face mask to prevent virus transmission, was advised to practice different social distancing measures, and were to comply with "whimsical" venue capacity numbers, aimlessly "plucked out of thin air." Another example of developing duality in society. This split in society was worsening faster than ever before. Just how much this will be reflected in future voting patterns, remains to be seen.

Success rates in mitigating the spread of the disease, were also different in left and right-controlled regions of the world. Was the type of regionalised governance, a factor in overall wellbeing? It could be argued quite convincingly (especially in America), that areas with hard lockdowns fared better, but unfortunately, the greater the lockdown, the more economic hardship was thrust upon the local economy. Regrettably, not too much emphasis was placed on age, climate, geographical location, and incumbent health of infected patients. Scientists and our leaders were more concerned with the "you know what impact." Yep, "dollars and the strength of the economy!"

There is significant growing resentment too, at the over-reaction to the virus, as projected infection and mortality rates, were nowhere near the level scientists had initially predicted. Had the economy been wrecked in a gross over-reaction to a perceived danger? The one "saving grace," was that Australia had dodged a bullet on comparison mortality rates. The Scott Morrison led, Liberal government, is to be commended in its response to limiting our infection rates. So far. At the time of writing, the same cannot be said for the Dan Andrews led, State Labor handling of affairs in Victoria.

As usual, there was the predictable "scare-mongering" and "alarmism" by the media. The media were quick to report daily increases in case numbers, but conveniently overlooked the very low mortality rates. This alarmism, propagated by the media, health experts, and senior politicians, is bordering on totalitarian behaviour. Their attempts to catastrophize the pandemic, no doubt added to the hysterics of government officials, conditioned personal reactions, and adversely influenced anxiety levels of the populace.

Governments now had an effective means of "controlling" the populace. This was certainly "going to their heads." Their sense of power was multiplied. Nowhere more so, than in Victoria where the Dan

Andrews-led, State Labor (socialists) Government, went to extremes in locking down the region as needed. "Control freak" springs to mind. They had the power to dictate how many patrons a venue could admit to its premises on a daily basis. A gross over-reaction to an unknown virus, and certainly an over-reach of their governing rights.

There was also concern at the recording and reporting of deaths. Notably, co-morbidity (where people suffer two different illnesses simultaneously), allowed those with an agenda, to inflate statistics in order to once again support a narrative. Many people dying from cancer or who were afflicted by other morbid illnesses for instance, had their actual death later attributed to covid-19, instead of their pre-existing ailment. This inflated mortality statistics, thereby supporting government agendas, and also providing a defence for their actions and social distancing measures. More homogenizing?

The governments "were damned if they did, and damned if they didn't." They got criticised for excessive expenditure on one hand, and criticised for not doing enough, to protect health and lives on the other. The whole pandemic had been weaponised, especially by those of the left.

For leading Western nations such as Australia, the UK, and the USA, the economic prudence that had given their respective governments political strength, had to be abandoned, in order to prevent the total collapse of their economies. The left was rejoicing, and their media buddies had a field day, highlighting the economic woes that were following. "Talk about taking the piss!"

The problem now, is "reigning in" the excessive spending through support packages. The populace, willing recipients of stimulus payments, are facing an end to their payments, and yet they still face unemployment in record numbers. This is going to compound the social unease already prevalent in society, in the ongoing culture wars.

While the virus is still ravaging the rest of the world, there is a desperate need to re-invigorate the struggling economies. Otherwise, unemployment, poverty, rising social unrest, depression, and even suicide, will do more damage in the long term than the virus ever did. Clearly though, the world is teetering on the edge of an economic abyss, with record debt, and record unemployment. Social unrest has even gone up another notch in recent times, as the speed of opening up the economy is frustratingly, deemed too slow.

Predictably, just as societies were lifting restrictions, the left and their biased media friends, had even began to re-address their climate concerns, as well as fears of a second wave of the virus. The clear skies reportedly created from economies shutting down industry and manufacturing, had given the left renewed impetus, on highlighting just how bad rampant capitalism had been for the environment. Entirely predictable in their relentless march to the extreme left, and in their quest for power.

On a positive note, the virus did do the whole world a couple of massive favours. Firstly, it highlighted the ineffectiveness of the World Health Organisation (WHO), and its charter. Likewise, the state of readiness to deal with a future serious pandemic, was hopelessly exposed in most Western nations. Important lessons were learnt on the need to have redundant reserves of medical infrastructure and supplies.

The greatest favour though, was the "wake-up call" the virus gave, about just how over-dependent countries had become on trading with China. In the early onset of the virus, Chinese nationals in Australia and other nations, had begun purchasing, stock-piling, and exporting to China, all available facemasks, surgical gloves, protective clothing, and hand sanitizers. It was as if Chinese nationals knew beforehand, just how bad things would become. This resulted in difficulty for the rest of the world in treating the disease, and in preventing its spread due to a shortage of protective equipment.

Suspicion grew at the true motives of the CCP, and the arrogant, obnoxious behaviour of some of their "ex-pats" around the world. It seems that the tentacles of the CCP have infiltrated every corner of the globe. Whilst their expansionist and aggressive tactics are causing concern in the South Pacific region, their dubious efforts to control and suppress the flow of information, has also "set tongues wagging."

Western efforts to identify the initial outbreak of the virus (identifying patient zero can aid in vaccine creation), have been stonewalled by CCP officials. There is high-level deceit, denial, and refusal, to let foreign investigators into Wuhan. In retaliation, they have also imposed trade sanctions on those seeking answers, in an effort to weaken them economically. The CCP wants to rule the world. As is the case with any bully, you cannot "kowtow" to them; you do have to stand up to them.

As earlier chapters highlighted, World Wars have been fought over the need to suppress rampant communism. Western nations are united in this battle, and have all realised their own personal over-dependence on China for trade. Caught up in capitalism and its virtues, they were "hypocritically" unconcerned, that a large proportion of their GDP was obtained from trade with China. The covid-19 virus border closures, have rammed home nationalism, and the need to look after and cater for oneself, rather than rely on cheap imports from China.

As the world was moving on from the first wave of covid-19, we were all to witness the distressing, accidental death in police custody, of a black individual in Minneapolis (USA). The death of George Floyd, as he was being "knelt on" while being arrested, was captured on film and quickly uploaded for broadcast all over the world. There was rightly, universal and widespread condemnation of what had occurred. But this did not prevent mass protests worldwide, the likes of which, the world had never seen. And the world saw as one, the extent of the divide, that had emerged between left and right. A pretty picture it was not.

8.4 Antifa emerges from the shadows

Antifa are a far-left, diverse array of autonomous groups, who seek to impose their political philosophy through non-violent and violent actions, rather than through policy reform. They are globalised, networked, decentralised, and violent. Antifa infiltrate peaceful protest actions through digital activism and militancy, in order to instigate the use of force by police. They are anarchists who seek to incite a backlash against the government. Their enemy in the twenty-first century, is capitalism, and those of the right who enjoy the fruits of an ordered democratic society.

Former United States President Theodore Roosevelt, described anarchists as "the enemy of humanity, the enemy of all mankind, and are a deeper degree of criminality than any other."

Jason Thomas (writer, Daily Telegraph 2020) likened antifa to how our immune systems work. They represent a "virus embedded within a host, that has the aim of creating a hyper-immune response. In other words, your own immune system becomes the killer." They seek to destabilise and topple governments from within.

They will employ any means necessary to achieve their objective, and often hijack seemingly irrelevant protests just to make a point. Anywhere, there is media reporting on a protest, you can expect antifa members to turn up, then mingle with the often, peaceful protesters and then finally "agitate" to stir up proceedings.

This was especially true in the protests that followed the death of George Floyd in Minneapolis. There was widespread outrage at the way this black individual was subdued as he resisted his arrest. Unfortunately, due to an alleged potential mix of illegal drugs in his system, and the deplorable manner in which a knee was applied to the lateral, rear of his neck, Mr Floyd's brain was starved of oxygen and he passed away. Despite the arresting officers being charged, hundreds of thousands exercised their right to protest this "black death in custody."

Once again, the lefties were not about "to look a gift horse in the mouth." Antifa and other social groups turned this into a "Black Lives Matter" (BLM) rally. Every protester had a mobile phone and images were quickly uploaded around the world. What started in Minneapolis, spread to other States of America within days, and to the rest of the world within a week. The world had gone mad.

The vast majority of protesters were peaceful, law-abiding folk, who were as frustrated at the covid-19 lockdown, as they were at the conduct of the arresting officers in Minneapolis. The concern for all governments, politicians, policy legislators, and police officials, was the magnitude of the turn outs, even during a pandemic, when lock downs and social distancing measures were supposedly in place. Would this trigger a second wave of the virus? Nations had been "flattening the curve" (rate of infection spread) which would see the virus contained and hopefully eradicated.

What it did expose however, was the bias, hypocrisy, the hidden agenda of the left, and the bias within certain sections of the media. Despite some protesters wearing face masks, many were not, thereby putting themselves and others, in danger of contracting the virus and even spreading it.

Mainstream society was also appalled at the fact so many were worshipping and idolising a man who had an "extensive criminal record", and who had been resisting arrest at the time of his unfortunate passing. This man had been in jail six times prior to his attempted arrest. His last sentence, which was for five years, was for an armed break and enter, where he pointed a gun against the body of a pregnant woman. This man was no angel, not of good character, and certainly not a good citizen. But as we continually see, this was blindly overlooked, as the left had weaponised the whole affair, and they were not about to "let up."

This protest was supposed to be about the death of one black man, of dubious character, who had broken the law yet again. The "Black Lives Matter" movement (BLM), turned this into their own battle against the seeming "injustice" that all indigenous members of society are subjected to. They were crazed in their defiance of covid-19 lockdown laws, and were determined to "milk" all the media exposure they could. The truth once again, mattered little, as they sought to divide people on race.

In America, in 2019, there were 1,004 people shot by a police officer, of which forty-one were unarmed. Of those shootings, thirty were fatal. Of the fatal shootings, ten were black victims, twenty were white victims. A more staggering number is, eighty-nine police officers were killed in the line of duty in 2019. So, if anyone should be vocal or rioting over rights, it should be the police. Where was the outcry for the white victims or the police victims?

In Australia, "Black Lives Matter" rallies were relatively peaceful, although they were unauthorised (making them illegal) and again, held during the pandemic. Indeed, at the time of writing, some protesters have since been infected by the virus, and a second wave of the virus has engulfed Victoria. The health risks of protesting, were "glossed over" by the protest organisers.

Here too, placards reading "432" were hoisted aloft by the protesters, in reference to the 432 indigenous Aboriginals who have died in police custody. Another misconception perpetrated by the left and their antagonistic friends, antifa. They were implying that all these deaths were the fault of the police. This was an outright lie and yet, so many were perpetuating the untruth.

This is supported by the findings of the Royal Commission into Aboriginal Deaths in Custody (1987-91). Instigated after an unusually high number of Aboriginal deaths in custody, the report concluded that Aborigines were not subject to abuse, neglect or racism, at the hands of police officers. Only one percent of these Aboriginal deaths were due to excessive man-handling issues by police officers.

The vast majority were due to natural causes, suicide, drug overdoses, and assaults by other indigenous detainees. But again, the socialist left had an agenda where the "truth didn't matter." The world saw one black man die at the hands of the police, and as far as the left was concerned, that is how all black men are treated. "One swallow does not make a summer." It was an over-reaction, and an appalling display by many of the protesters. But it served to finally awaken those on the right, who have been in a slumber, basking in the glory of recent election victories around the world.

The left has grown restless to a level never seen before. They have become immune from the truth. If you are a "woke lefty," you are a correct thinker, you can do whatever you like, say what you wish, and break the law with no repercussions.

If you are from the right, and you don't agree with them (on any matter, regardless of how trivial), you are a racist. They have drawn a line in the sand. Any minority group that feels persecuted, has joined forces with the lefties and together they have "circled the wagons."

In America, the Donald Trump Derangement Syndrome was merely a precursor when you look at it. It is nothing more than a blatant denial of the 2016 U.S. general election result. The lefty Democrats have been upset ever since. When their impeachment plans failed, they quickly jumped onto the virus pandemic, as a means to over-throw the duly-elected President. As discussed, they even wish for an economic collapse to wreak havoc on America, just so that they can campaign on Trump's failed economic policies at the upcoming 2020 election.

Think I am joking? Look at the behaviour of antifa at the protests in America. Not content with peaceful protesting, ring leaders are at the front of the marches. They "antagonise and goad" the police, eagerly seeking a reaction to incite their audience. They are armed at marches with backpacks containing communications, gas masks, first aid kits, milk (to cleanse eyes afflicted by tear gas and pepper spray), marbles (to roll on the ground to make police horses lose their footing), spray-paint (for graffiti), accelerants, fireworks, and matches. Arson, looting, and general lawlessness, are a feature of their anarchistic behaviour.

They cowardly "run with the foxes, but hunt with the hounds." Once the police are outnumbered or lose control, they begin to run amok, inciting fellow protesters to engage in similar activity. In the BLM protests, they embarked on a looting, arson, graffiti, and wanton vandalism spree. Encouraged by the fact the police were often ordered to stand down by lefty senior government officials, their protests quickly morphed into a dangerous "defund the police" rally. This was echoed right across many American cities, and also in large capital cities throughout the rest of the world.

The call went out around the world to "defund the police" and then it was elaborated on, by demands that all policing be abolished. Seriously! An end to law and order? How would society exist and remain viable, if there was no law and order? Again, when asked about this by news reporters on the streets, many replied that they "didn't know." The protesters were just hellbent on drawing our attention to "any perceived inequalities in society" that they could think of.

Ironically, "defund the police" can be viewed as the "ultimate compliment" to capitalism. Do the radical socialists know "deep down" that they are doomed to failure? It is as if they know their only chance of a progressive state, is to dismantle the law and order which preserves capitalism and democracy.

Most interesting of all though, was that the severity of the damage and intensity of the protests, was greatest in cities that were governed locally by leftist politicians and mayors. It was obvious that these city law makers did nothing to quell the protests. They were more intent on politicising the events, in order to harm the re-election prospects of the right Republican President Donald Trump.

They were happy to let "mob rule" engulf their city streets. Socialism in its purity. While the anarchists were revelling in the mayhem they created, the rest of society could only look on and watch. The media were having a field day. They were even too blinded by their own left bias, to notice that some of their own reporters in the field were also being attacked.

But it doesn't have to be this way. The difference between capitalism (right) and socialism (left) was on full display for all to see. If you did not know the difference before these events, you surely did now. It is wise to study an adversary and know your enemy. We can now all go to the ballot box in the future, knowing just how important our vote really is, and what it stands for.

The protests in America reached their crescendo, in Seattle, of all places. Just as the protests were running out of steam for all but the anarchists, protesters decided to take over six or seven square blocks in the middle of down-town Seattle. They took control of the local police precinct, as officers were ordered to stand down by the woke local mayor. The little region became known as "Chaz" (Capitol Hill Autonomous Zone). It was coordinated by armed anarchists of antifa, who barricaded the zone and prevented police access. To date, the woke lefty mayor Jenny Durkin could only describe it as a "love-in," and she has done nothing to restore peace or law and order to the region.

It serves as a tiny example of the impoverished, lawless quality of life that would be endured under a socialist political system. President Trump has offered to retake the streets on behalf of local officials, but once again they are refusing assistance, instead preferring to politicise the matter. "Never interrupt your enemy while they are making a mistake."

Perhaps Mr Trump is doing the world a favour by letting the lefties "shoot themselves in the foot," by trying to control a region using pure socialist means. If we didn't already know it, we can now see what a society bereft of law and order, would look like. At the time of writing, police were not responding to calls for assistance from inside this little enclave. Those left within the boundaries, had no one to turn to in their time of need. There have been armed holdups and two murders committed to date, without response from law enforcement. "The novelty just might be wearing off."

In just three weeks, a downtown part of Seattle was rendered unliveable. Covered in graffiti and littered by debris, handfuls of homeless people were left to sit around amongst their own excrement, and ponder just how wonderful a socialist "utopia" would be. Criminalised warlords controlled the streets, heavily armed, and safe in the knowledge that there would be no police reprisals for their actions. You have to wonder who was paying for their reticulated water, sewer, and electrical services. It would only be a matter of time before these were disconnected.

The level of derangement of the left knows no bounds. Momentum gained from the BLM protests, soon morphed into a worldwide woke attack on anything that was perceived racist or likely to offend. The politically correct left, went on a worldwide spree of erasing all historical sources of inequality. Statues around the world became the target of graffiti, defacing, removal, destruction, or dismantling. If one person took offense, then it was time for that statue to go. Absolute stupidity, which was further enhanced, by lefty local councils assisting illegal efforts to destroy our historical past.

The keyboard warriors (senders of faceless malicious emails or posts on social platforms) of the left, then set their sights on anyone who disagreed with their views. The woke don't like to be offended. Or is it just "sour grapes," because they know they haven't got the numbers to assume power in democratic elections? Manufacturers and producers of all goods and services that could be perceived as unfairly treating minorities, were subjected to hate emails, and threats to boycott their products.

Coco pops, Coon cheese, Colonial beer, Johnson and Johnson white skin cleaner were a few of many products targeted, not because there was anything wrong with them, but merely the fact that the activist lefties took offense to their brand names. Absolutely ludicrous. But just how serious, were the threats to force these items to be removed from shelves? Unfortunately, those on the right, concerned that these email attacks would lower their sales, (and thereby profits) were quick to bow to their demands.

The woke lefties also used anonymous protest groups to bombard advertisers, to encourage boycotts of any product or good they did not like. Talk-back radio hosts have been threatened, just because they denounce some of the actions of those on the left. In reply, activists targeted any sponsors of their radio shows, resulting in a loss of advertising revenue for radio station owners.

"The mob" as they are now referred to as, have been allowed to run riot, unrestrained by law enforcement, and it is having an unnerving effect on social cohesion in society. One thing is for sure. The combined effect of measures to combat climate change, the covid-19 pandemic, and the uprising in social unrest arising from the BLM protests, have been a triple hammer-blow to the state of world affairs.

Countries founded on strong capitalist beliefs are on their knees economically, with massive debts and severe recessions or depression looming. To complicate matters, the socialists buoyed by the impending collapse of society as we know it, are "circling like vultures" waiting to pick up the pieces. Their socialist "utopia" is within their reach.

For the rest of us, it can be seen as their quest for power. Unable to attain power through elections, the centre-leftists have had to form coalitions with Green and extreme-left political parties, in order to obtain majorities. But they have sold out their identity and what they stand for. They have "got into bed with the enemy." It had been a case of "out of sight, out of mind" for many decades, but the events of the last few years, have a lot of people scared at the ramifications of impending socialism.

9
Navigating the Point of No Return

9.1 Light your own fire

Never in our history, has the world been confronted with such a dangerous cocktail of colliding events. Knowing the difference between right and left, and the voting repercussions that come with it, can influence our future stability, and dare I say it, existence. Our children, should we continue to benefit from continued economic growth, will have to fight this battle for their own children in years to come. I can only emphasize the importance of self-reliance in teaching our young what has been discussed in this book.

Sometimes in life, you have to "light your own fire" and dig yourself out of a hole. The economic mess engulfing the world, can only be fixed by electing political parties that nurture and encourage economic growth. Capitalism is a proven means of increasing wealth for all, even if there can be a slower trickle-down redistribution of wealth through social welfare.

Pandering to leftist, socialist minority groups, does nothing to build an economy, but rather placates a privileged few. "You reap what you sow." Failure to educate our youth on the importance of voting wisely, will result in us having no one to blame for our demise except ourselves. The choice has never been clearer.

Venezuela on a national level, is the obvious, modern-day example of failed socialism. But look at recent events closely, and see how local regions have fared under the authoritative control of lefty local governments. In America, the lefty states of Seattle, Washington, California, Chicago, Baltimore, New York, Detroit, Oregon, and Minneapolis, all have declining law and order standards. There is rising inequality and massive issues of unemployment, homelessness, civil unrest, and poverty in these lefty states.

In Australia, the lefty states of Victoria, South Australia, the Northern Territory and Queensland all have massive debt levels, rising unemployment, and growing inequality. They are governed in a dubious manner by socialists, hellbent on maintaining power, even if it means financial ruin for the local population. In their socialist ways, they seem more intent on righting social inequalities, than they do on addressing the financial issues facing the locals.

They are clearly not delivering on the economic front, and are wasting precious taxpayer dollars on trivial social equality issues. The poor, quiet man on the street is angry, and sick of not being listened to. An upheaval is needed, and it can only come from the ballot box. And with the lefties wanting open borders to bring in more left-leaning future voters, there has never been more important time to preserve the strength and base size of the right-leaning voters.

Any self-respecting citizen can see what needs to be done to fix the mire. The time has come for us to "put our money where our mouth is." Citizens in lefty states have to learn to "do the hard yards themselves." They should be electing a conservative state government that can deliver on reforms, and not rely on handouts from the federal government in the traditional, socialist way.

One problem confronting right-leaning voters, is the high number of public servants and union-affiliated voters in lefty regions. While they are "suckling at the public teat," they are unlikely to vote against their lefty leaders. Conservative voters cannot rely on others "to do the heavy lifting," if they want their standards of living to remain. They have to stand and defend the institutions of our society that have given us such a privileged existence. In times to come, this may require more than just the odd vote at a ballot box.

It is time for our talented young men and women to have the courage to enter politics and fight for the traditional values held dearly by all. We have to recognise that senior political members of both political persuasions have become clouded in their judgement. There is no more room for "wishy washy, sit on the fence" types. All Western nations are crying out for a new crop of young political aspirants eager to learn from our predecessors and take society to the next level. Fortunately, there is a sprinkling of young talent emerging through the ranks. Let's hope they know their history.

9.2 Forthcoming resilience of the right

Most of all "have faith." Regardless of your religious denomination, or even political persuasion, one cannot argue that rampant economic growth and comparative world stability, have not existed since the advent of nuclear weapons at the end of World War Two.

Living under the shadow of potential nuclear Armageddon, nations have continued to co-exist, despite the odd border skirmish. Society has become multi-cultural, and there is significant tolerance of religious differences in most regions. In light of recent events however, to continue to prosper and maintain stability, education needs to be re-prioritised. Upholding education standards enables history to be grasped, learnt from, and improved upon.

The key to a "societal reset" is education. "How boring," you all say. It is not a "sexy" solution to todays' woes. We have time to work on this because socialism also takes many years to fully manifest itself into society. We need to remember that "throwing money at a problem" usually only results in the problem getting bigger. The behaviour this creates, is human nature.

There needs to be a push to "incentivise" teaching as a profession. To attract a better quality of university graduate that will want to pursue teaching as a career. A balance needs to be struck between left and right-leaning beliefs within the teaching fraternity.

Education, be it from unionised left or right-leaning teachers, is vital, as long as objectivity is encouraged and observed. Children should be free to formulate their own opinions on all matters, including the lefty trojan horse "climate change." The "courage of conviction" should be fostered in all future generations. To "stand up and argue for what you believe in," should not lead to one being condemned as racist.

There is a recognised need to improve on our education standards, which have been in decline in recent years. The current curriculum needs a serious overhaul, as too many leftist agendas have found their way into the curriculum. For example, some Australian states were incredibly, on the verge of introducing studies on Greta Thunberg, the media "darling" of the left.

The fact that she speaks nonsense half the time, didn't seem to deter those wanting her ramblings to become gospel. Fortunately, common sense prevailed, and study of her offerings has been curtailed by senior education ministers. But this does serve to highlight the manner in which the left has infiltrated all levels of education.

There have even been attempts to discuss the BLM movement in English classes. Who is politicizing this? Which government ministers are condoning this? Are our children being "indoctrinated" as it now seems?

The left has "woke up," while those of the right need to "wakeup." We cannot "rest on our laurels" and marvel at the fine society capitalism has created. This battle has to take place in our educational institutions. Why are the left allowed to ban studies in the history of Western democracy? Why are the left permitting Chinese "Confucius Institutes" on university campuses? The left is in a battle, but the right must not allow them to win the war. Should they prevail, society as we know it, is doomed to fail.

Perhaps our leaders and their followers, could "take a leaf out of the book" of young Australian, Drew Pavlou. This fine young man was a student of The University of Queensland. He stood up to the rise of Chinese influence on campus, and protested against the loss of rights of the citizens of Hong Kong, as they came under Chinese rule. A shame that he was suspended by the University for his efforts.

But the whole debacle, further highlights the intrusion of the CCP into Australian society. It is now readily apparent where the University of Queensland gets it's "bread buttered." More hypocrisy from our leaders. It can be a hard battle to wage, when some of our elites have their allegiances torn between their patriotism towards Australia, and their economic prudence fostered by China.

It gets even worse. You now get Green politicians calling for financial support for visiting Chinese students. Not only do these students fill university spaces that could be taken by Australian students, but asking the Australian taxpayer to fund Chinese student education is incredulous. What are the Greens thinking? Then again, we shouldn't be surprised by their rantings. Afterall, they refuse to adopt nuclear energy as a means of power generation, when we have the richest uranium reserves in the world. That's right, Australia is the only G20 nation to ban uranium. Go figure! No wonder we are all going broke.

Unfortunately, inequality in wealth distribution, does hinder the ability of some, to share in education opportunities in different geographic regions. That said, with this connection between economic growth and education standards, it begs the question "what came first? The chicken or the egg?" Is an advanced education system created by national economic wealth, or was the wealth created by an educated, democratic society?

A key component of education is literacy. Mastery of the English language, and the ability to write, have allowed mankind to excel in noble pursuits such as science, history, and the arts. Numeracy skills have allowed advances in mathematics, science, chemistry, communications, and information technology.

With sound knowledge, our ability to communicate and acquire further knowledge, was aided and abetted by the ordered society that ensued. Growth in the wealth that followed, enabled further research and development, which then rapidly expanded the rise of technology, as seen in the industrial revolution. Education has a multiplier effect on wealth and as such, is the key to our future.

Those of the right can no longer afford to sit back quietly. They have to get on the front foot and confront the aggressors of the left. Some of these battles will have to be fought in the classroom and in our university lecture theatres. This ethos, has to be instilled in our future voters by parents, rather than relying on lefty teachers, either at secondary or tertiary levels of education.

Our students should be encouraged to challenge what they are being taught in the classroom. They have the right to question, debate, argue, and refute information that is currently presented to them in a subjective manner.

As parents, if you do not agree with the gender studies in our primary schools, the time has come to march down to the principal's office and vent your disgust. To sit there meekly, and accept what is preached, only gives the left more strength. They revel in the lack of fight from those on the right.

Afterall, it is better "to die on your feet, than it is to live on your knees." At the moment, the "right" seem content to live on their knees. Maybe, that is why so many have surrendered and "taken a knee," in what they claim, is "solidarity against racism."

But then again, those of the sensible centre, and the right, are renowned for their common-sense attitude, and their support of the right to peaceful protest. In recent times, they have acknowledged the protests at BLM and at social distancing measures. They have shown solidarity with those who feel aggrieved, but that does not mean society has to meekly "rollover" and give the socialists what they want.

Political leaders of both political persuasions, need to stand up and be counted, instead of "beating around the bush" when discussing current issues. Those of the centre-left, now have to condemn the appalling behaviour of radical protesters and their own supporters, who are engaged in this battle with the frontline police in all nations. They have become so obsessed with the uprising and their rising poll popularity, that they are "killing the goose that laid the golden egg."

Unfortunately, the current left socialist leaders Joe Biden (USA) and Anthony Albanese (Australia), have both taken the same disastrous path that Jeremy Corbyn (UK) embarked upon. Mr Corbyn steered the British Labour Party to the hard-left, with disastrous consequences. Given what is unfolding around the world at present, it is hard to understand the logic of taking the Democrats (USA) and Labor (Australia), to the far-left. This may placate the extremist, anarchistic socialists, but it will destroy what little economic security our Western nations have left, should they be elected to govern.

Adopting the lefty ideology of green energy, is overly expensive, and will result in massive rises in power costs for the nations that embark on these measures. The willingness to adopt "open borders," will deplete the health and education resources of these Western nations. As for the "defunding of police?" Well, that policy will only serve to leave the general population at the mercy of the lawless anarchists. That is sure to be a vote winner, come election time. Not!

In this globalised world, "one size fits all." The arguments of the left in America, are quickly "latched onto" down under, and play out in the same manner. When governments start to lose the respect of their citizens, adherence to the law quickly diminishes, and the economic rot sets in. Then, when you start to see the decline of education, health service provision, personal safety, law and order, economic prosperity, and the truth, society heads down the sorry path to ruin. "Socialism" grows in strength, but this only serves to provide a "false dawn." Then, the last throes of an ordered society, will see widespread poverty, and eventually, a lack of access to food and drinking water.

At the time of writing, Democrat nominee in America, Joe Biden was embracing "the Squad" members, who are calling for the dismantling of the American Constitution. What is he thinking? Or is the lust for power so blinding, that he cannot see the damage the Democrats are wreaking on America? Or has he been rendered a mere puppet, too scared to stand up against the extremists? Looks to me, like he has opted for the hypocritical stance of ignoring their behaviour, in order to secure their vote. God help us if the Democrats win the 2020 election. All this will have achieved, is the dangerous "rewarding of bad behaviour." Good luck "turning the tap off" after the election.

If the progressives cannot control the vitriol, antagonistic behaviour, and sheer aggression of their supporters, they have little chance of managing an economy. They seem incapable of standing up to their own. As we have seen, it is this phenomenon which causes revolutions to implode, as factions eventually turn on each other.

Our current crop of political leaders all have some room for improvement. The progressives could do well to move their parties back to the sensible centre. The socialist far-left radicals, are seeking to destroy capitalism and will ultimately, also destroy lefty political parties, as they wage their war on us. Leaders also have to recognise, that they have allowed an unprecedented "duality" to pervade our society.

The law, the truth, and respect, are being applied differently to people of left or right persuasion. The wealthy are issued more fines, as authorities know they have the means to pay the penalty. The less fortunate are having their penalties waived. Yes, even in Australia, if you are in receipt of government stimulus payments (in response to covid-19), you don't have to pay road tolls, whilst any outstanding infringement notices are also being quashed.

In parts of America governed locally by lefties, criminals charged with crime, are now being released back onto the streets without bail. There is no incentive to abide by the law any more, as deterrents have been removed. This duality is dangerous, and if allowed to continue, will soon give rise to a whole new level of inequality and animosity between members of society.

This duality is further enhanced by wokeness, which is also weakening law and order efforts. When police seek the perpetrators of crime, they are now not allowed to describe the skin colour of who it is they are looking for! What about their height? Is this "heightism" and bias against tall or short people? Common sense has "left the building," as equality knows no bounds.

Our leaders from the right, can see this happening, but to date, some appear reluctant to address the issue. Others are having their amendments to laws blocked in the lower houses of parliament by minority groups.

Recent emergency stimulus payments, have helped to slow the calamitous economic impact of the covid-19 pandemic, but with so much money being given to those who have lost their jobs, it is like a "socialist Christmas." Millions are in receipt of these payments (in Australia and in overseas countries too). The Australian Liberal Prime Minister's popularity has surged, while real unemployment figures have been hidden and temporarily deferred. But, "there is a sting in the tail!"

Massive, unprecedented levels of national debt have been accrued, and it is a debt that society will have to eventually confront and repay. Likewise, many workers previously on low pay or minimal hours, are reluctant to return to the workforce. This again, exemplifies one of the problems with socialism, in that it does not create incentive to work hard. Another "wake up call," on the dangers of socialism, that we don't need.

Our right-leaning leaders, are also guilty of hypocrisy too! As we are having to confront the growing menace of China, our conservative governments have to acknowledge the fact, that we are over-reliant on trade, with the Western world's "New Cold War" enemy. Hopelessly outnumbered by a country of 1.4 billion inhabitants, it is going to take a willing coalition of Western nations to confront together, the aggressive Chinese actions, tirades, trade embargoes, and sanctions. We need to remember, that current CCP actions are intended to deflect attention away from the fact, that their own economy is retracting and in trouble. Afterall, it is the "communist way" to project strength, rather than concede that all is not well internally.

For the West, without an aggressive determination to engage in a trade war, there will come again, a need to implement policies that encourage the local manufacture of currently-imported Chinese goods.

This will be no easy feat. Unions demanding ever-increasing wage rises, and ridiculously high electricity costs (which will sky-rocket when renewable energy gets implemented), will leave Australian manufacturing uncompetitive. Compare this to our Chinese "friends," who have a massive cheap labour force, and who are building 273 new coal-fired power stations. We are seriously sending ourselves broke. And the woke brigade are encouraging this. Why?

Apart from the current state of affairs, rural Australia has also been crippled with droughts (that are a part of the cyclical "El Nino" weather phenomenon). There have been repeated calls, to build more dams to harvest flood waters. There has also been dismay, at the lack of foresight, into the planning of future dam infrastructure. One has to wonder; maybe our conservative leaders "know something we don't."

The truth is, the Chinese are buying up a lot of the freehold farming lots in our finest farmland areas. Why should Mr Taxpayer pay exorbitant amounts to irrigate the land now owned by foreigners? That's one topic for another day. To delve into it further, is to possibly be labelled racist.

Australia's hypocritical economic reliance on Chinese students paying to study in Australia, and the exporting of resources to China, cannot be expected to continue if tensions rise further. It will come down to a simple choice for elected leaders. Do we risk our sovereignty (as China seeks to overtake us), in the pursuit of dollars which improve our economic wellbeing?

To "stick your head in the sand," and not see what China is really up to, is a dangerous thing to do. Fortunately, our "five eyes" leaders are awake to them, and things are about to change. Perhaps this is why China is starting to "up the ante" on rhetoric about the growing international concern at their expansionist policies. Afterall, the CCP hates nothing more, than to "lose face" in front of its own people.

Our conservative leaders "need to grow some balls." We had their back at recent elections. It is time for them to "repay the favour." They have to enforce the law and order that has been the backbone of Western civilisation. They have to call out and renounce, this invasion of wokeness into society, by adjusting federal legislation.

The Racial Discrimination Act (18c), needs to be amended, to address the wokeness permeating society. The general public are fed up with it. Lawmakers need to get tough on dissenters and law breakers through the court systems. Current fines are no longer deterrents to radical, dangerous behaviour. If politicians are not strong enough or willing to defend the constituents, then they have failed in their charter. It is time for them to be removed and replaced, if they can't "cut the mustard."

Our front line of defence, the police, should be given new powers and greater protection, rather than be defunded or abolished. Personally, I do not know what our leaders are waiting for. Yes, I do. Political correctness is stifling our leader's ability "to call a spade a spade." They are afraid of being seen as "un-woke." It is no wonder, that these days, victims of crime are treated worse than the perpetrators of crime. Remember Malcolm X's words?

Like all countries, many of our leading politicians, have their own motivations for their actions. Gone are the days of integrity. We the constituents, are being used in the election cycle for political gain, then thrown back on the scrap heap. Corruption, backroom deals, and dishonoured election promises, have become the norm. As Western governments have become more impotent, China has quietly grown in strength and stature, to become an international menace.

An emerged superpower, they are now threatening trade wars and are involved in border skirmishes. The CCP are lying to the world about the pandemic, as their behaviour has caused world economies to teeter on the verge of collapse. It appears that The United Nations and The World Health Organisation, have both been taken over by CCP interests, to the detriment of the free world. Concerningly, it seems that no country, has the "stomach" to call out this behaviour, except for Donald Trump's America. Perhaps a collective worldwide-approach is necessary. Afterall, this is what it took, to win the first two World Wars.

Fortunately, there is a growing consensus, to reject the use of Chinese communications technology in Western nations. Suspicion levels have mounted about the Chinese using these means to "spy" on foreign nations. "Huawei," a leading telecommunication and technology company, is losing its world market share, as Western governments turn their back on them, over mistrust of the Chinese Communist Party. Tiktok, owned and operated by Chinese interests, is now being banned in many nations throughout the world. This was due to concerns over its data collection capabilities and privacy invasion.

Recent escalations in international tension have occurred, as cyber-attacks have been perpetrated on leading Western government agencies. In the old days, these would have been considered an "act of war." To date, no one is calling this out, even though everyone seems to know, where to "point the finger."

These foreign incursions to Western political systems, are becoming a major distraction, as the Western nations have to fight social upheavals within their own borders. In Australia, there is growing concern at the level of foreign ownership of resources. Whether it be the leasing of the Port of Darwin, a greater share of water allocation on the Murray River,

Victorian "belt and road" initiatives, or rising home ownership, nothing compares to the danger of Chinese people entering our parliament. Even though they are Australian citizens, the Chinese have infiltrated our universities and energy sectors with disastrous results. The recent Chinese infiltration of Hong Kong, has demonstrated the real threat of the Chinese Communist Party, and revealed their true motives.

The Chinese want to rule and control the world. They are attempting to destabilise Western political systems. It is no coincidence, that their aspirations are riding on the back of the socialist uprising. Afterall, communism is the end game of socialism.

In Australia, Labor (left) members of parliament have been siding with China and praising the CCP leadership in their handling of the covid-19 pandemic. The Labor party has been accused of branch-stacking, in order to determine candidates for election, and then to win seats at elections. Does this branch-stacking, involve the use of local Chinese communities, to bolster the numbers of local Chinese candidates?

The Liberals (right) in Australia, really do have to stand up, or our nation and society is lost. Political correctness can no longer be used as a "cop out." Donald Trump stood up to this oppression in America, as he announced he was going to "drain the swamp." Whilst he can be "rough around the edges" in his demeanour and rhetoric, he is "fighting the fight" for those of the right. More of this "bravado" is needed.

The "swamp" is metaphorically, the malaise that was bringing America down, and is where socialism had begun to thrive. Mr Trump went "against the grain," by giving impetus to the free markets, and the economy, prior to the pandemic, responded. As the Trump Derangement Syndrome engulfed the American left, the anarchists descended on the carcass of the old Democratic party. They do not want a better America. They are only after power and rest assured; the individual American on the street, will be the greatest loser, if the Republicans under Trump, lose the next election in 2020.

The ironies and similarities of the socialists and Chinese, could not be more obvious. They are both after power, and they are hypocritical, in all of their behaviour. They seek the oppression of all in their way, by silencing their opponents, either by force (Chinese) or by wokeness and political correctness (lefties). They both manipulate the "hidden message" in what you see, read or hear. That point alone, should scare the "the living daylights" out of you!

Conservatives are going to have to stand up to socialism, not just at the ballot box, but in their everyday activities. They should not feel afraid to call out the bias they see emanating from the left. It can be daunting to stand up for your beliefs in a hostile environment. It can often be wise (and in extreme cases, physically safer), to back down on the rhetoric, but rather deliver your sermon at the ballot box. But beware! When socialists get into power, the ballot box can disappear altogether. As socialist systems inevitably collapse, corruption and lawlessness will be so rampant, a fair election will not be possible.

In the future, the method of conducting elections will come under increasing scrutiny. There is so much at stake, that stakeholders will go to great lengths to win the vote. Technology will advance efforts to "rig" mail ballot votes. Stringent identification will be required to ensure people only vote once. Electoral fraud will pose a future danger to counted results. The whole preferential voting system needs to be reviewed and overhauled, in order to prevent minority parties having the power to influence election outcomes. But, don't expect these issues to be fixed by socialist politicians.

Clearly, many on the right are "fighting the good fight" with dignity and respect. No need for violence or public demonstrations. Just a calm, orderly stroll to the polling booths on election day shall suffice. But be warned, in years to come this will not be enough.

A whole new generation of right-leaning voters have to be recruited, and made aware of the real conflict that will shape their lives. Unfortunately, many of our 16 to 19-year-olds have already had their brains subjected to socialist propaganda, so it is imperative that parents and peers set the record straight; to let them make their own objective, informed opinions.

"I am getting too old for this shit." This book is my contribution to the fight. Your contribution can be to read, understand, and convey the messages contained herein. Simple. "Life wasn't meant to be easy." It never will be. Our struggles will be worse though, if we have to live through a "Venezuela-style" collapse of society.

9.3 Bias, hypocrisy, racism and lies

The hypocritical left, is trying to control your thoughts and actions. Manipulating the media, distorting the truth, publishing fake polls, and lying to you. These are the tactics of the left delivered by their news buddies. They have been called out by Donald Trump as the broadcasters of "Fake News."

In recent times, the fake news brigade even fiddle numbers to justify their stance on the socialist narrative. Whenever there is a protest by the left, the lefty media mob "inflate" or "exaggerate" the number of participants, to trick you into believing this is the overall will of the people. Likewise, if the conservatives have a protest or march, the fake news mob, will deliberately fudge the participant numbers in a downward manner. They want you to feel in the minority. This is totalitarian behaviour.

It was the same, in the reporting coverage of recent election results in many countries. The mob was reporting that conservatives were heading to defeat on many occasions. Even as the votes were being counted, the mob were reporting that the left was marching to victory, when in reality, they were heading over a cliff. Can you see the pattern?

The ultimate betrayal of the people. The lefties want to destroy Western civilisation and capitalism. If they do, your safety, wealth and freedom are gone with it. They blame racism as the cause of inequality. Racism? Australia is a shining example of the success of a multi-cultural society. While people may choose to reside in enclaves due to socio-economic forces, there is tolerance of all ethnic, religious, and cultural differences.

When Cathy Freeman (Aboriginal) won gold (in the 400m track event) for Australia at the 2000 Olympics, there was not a "dry eye in the house." Black or white mattered little, as she was the pride of Australia. Since then, the only change has been the rise of socialism, not the rise of racism.

In America, if racism is such a problem, why are so many migrants trying to get "into" the country? African Americans, Latinos, Mexicans, and Asians, are all seeking their fortune in the "land of the free."

In 2019, Jussie Smollett, a famous dark-skinned actor claimed he was assaulted in a racially-motivated attack on the streets of Chicago. Yet, there is evidence to suggest that the attack was staged, and the accused offenders, were in fact paid by Jussie in a pre-coordinated attack. If racism is so rampant, why the need to fake a racially-motivated attack? Police investigations into this incident are ongoing, but there is no doubt that the final court ruling on this matter, will also cause further social unrest.

Most people do not have the time or place, to sit and watch full interviews of politicians in their press announcements. But if you do, take the time to listen to the soft questions put forward to the lefties, while those on the right are bombarded with questions that are often controversial and unanswerable. Such a clear and unfair bias.

In the United States, Joe Biden is seventy-seven and running for President in 2020, yet at the time of writing, he had not given one interview in eighty-two days. He is not fit to be the leader of the free world. His gaffes and lack of policy ideas have rendered him a "puppet" of the far-left extremists. Even his own Democrat Party thinks he "should be seen and not heard." A couple of poor-quality podcasts, was all he could offer the American public. His opponent, Mr Trump cannot seem to go ten minutes without demands for his time. Such hypocrisy and duality.

In other recent examples of this bias, CNN accused Covington Catholic High School student Nick Sandman of racism, just because he wore a Donald Trump "Make America Great Again" red cap. This poor young fellow merely stood his ground and smiled, while a native American protester banged his drum into the poor kids face. The kid's smirk, was deemed racist by CNN, and footage of this confrontation went all around the world. One of the CNN leading news broadcast anchor-men even suggested, that Nick had a face you could "smack."

CNN would not let up, on using this footage to incite hatred and divide the American people. Wisely, the young lad sued for defamation and was able to settle out of court for a handsome sum of money. You think CNN would learn. But no, during the covid-19 pandemic, they even broadcast a "staged" fake virus testing stand complete with actors, just to create the appearance of a situation out of control at the hands of Donald Trump. Talk about derangement! It is now a hyped-up paranoia that is out of control.

This is not a random, subjective view of affairs by the odd journalist or speaker of the left. Watch CNN for twenty-four hours, and you see that every headline has the same few words. Repeat a lie enough times and it becomes the truth. On any given day, you get repeatedly bombarded with the same jingo or three-word "slogan" to convert your way of thinking. "Impeachment bombshell," "believe all women," "Trump causes poisoning death," "Trump endangers America."

The "Trump Derangement Syndrome" was coined by his supporters, to discredit criticism of his actions, as a way of reframing the discussion, by suggesting that his opponents are incapable of accurately perceiving the world. CNN are clearly guilty of this, as they criticise anything and everything he does, perceiving it to be irrational. They have little regard for his policies, their success, nor the actions undertaken by his administration.

To emphasize this point, when Donald Trump ordered the air strikes that eliminated the world's leading terrorists al Baghdadi, Al-Rimi, and Soleimani, CNN ran headlines that stated "Donald Trump was taking America to war," and that Trump was even "racist." They actually chose to support the people of Iran, the sworn enemies of the United States. They are so intent on bringing down the American President, that they would willingly destroy the country, just so that they could be in power. You might think I am joking, but look at how Democrat mayors have let lawlessness destroy left-governed American cities.

Malcolm X warned us more than fifty years ago. The media is the most powerful entity on earth. They have the power to "make the innocent guilty and to make the guilty innocent." Their power gives them an image-making ability to control the minds of the masses. It can make the criminal look like he's the victim and make the victim look like he's the criminal. Just look at the George Floyd fiasco as a recent example of this. This is subversion of the minds and totalitarian behaviour. Maybe the media are the enemy and not the Chinese?

If you are not careful, the newspapers will have you hating the people who are being oppressed, and loving the people who are doing the oppressing. History is warning us. That is why the left are so quick to erase history and ignore the facts.

They are the masters of political correctness and instilling wokeness in order to control your behaviour. The woke brigade of the left have even taken to controlling how you discipline in your children. "You can't say this, you can't do that." You are not even allowed to "smack" your child as a discipline method. This weakens the ability to teach right from wrong.

The result is the current crop of poorly educated, law-breaking, disrespectful youth, running amok in society and joining the socialist cause. Wokeness and political correctness has fostered a new wave of hostility. The young are rejecting conventional beliefs, have no respect for the law, and are being brainwashed into despising all that Western society and capitalism have created.

Woke activists and the keyboard warriors are increasingly being seem as the non-contributors to society, who are now intent on disruptive behaviour by any means possible. They are weak, often jobless, and have no desire to work hard and get ahead. Their efforts to create equality, amount to little more than a race to the bottom. They are seeking to take away your wealth, your money, your safety. That way, everyone can be equal and all have nothing. Is that what you have worked hard all your life for?

Before they can go after your money, they are first taking away your freedom of speech. The loss of liberty, is weakening the institutions upon which the West was founded. Stable responsible government and the church are the first to go, along with the freedom to speak your mind. When you cannot refute an argument, all is lost.

They are getting louder, as governments seem unwilling to stand up to their undermining, aggressive tactics. You only have to look at the current offering of "weak-kneed" politicians, who seem unwilling to confront rising socialism. Certainly, no Winston Churchill types there. A cherished Prime Minister who led the United Kingdom to victory in World War Two, all memory of him is currently being hastily removed by the statue-destroying left.

Rather than get dejected at fighting a losing battle against socialism, one needs to step back and laugh at the ludicrous offerings from the socialists at the moment. It is no wonder education standards are diminishing when you look at the idiocy on display. Just yesterday (July 29, 2020), in America, Democrat house speaker Nancy Pelosi described Attorney General William Barr as a "Blob." Mr Barr had been addressing the Judiciary House Committee on his findings regarding Democrat behaviour since 2016. Nancy Pelosi was at her deranged best and showed the West, just how unhinged the Democratic party had become. Certainly not the behaviour, demeanour or language of someone representing a party that want to govern the United States.

Their agenda is no longer a secret, as they have recently become so unhinged, they ignore the truth and facts, and seek to destroy any history that ridicules their ideology. You need to draw strength from their bias, hypocrisy, and ignorance of the facts.

Their blatant disregard of historical records helps them perpetuate the global warming hoax. The idolisation of Greta Thunberg (a sixteen-year-old with learning and development difficulties) is embarrassing. Her lefty green activist parents have paraded her to the world, and her growing popularity has elevated her to "cult-like" status. A "messiah" on climate change? Please?

Where are the grown adults and scientists questioning her proclamations? This young girl preaches all things green and yet, hops onto carbon-emitting aeroplanes at the drop of a hat to promote the lefty narrative. Ask her a question about the facts and she becomes enraged with denial. Remember narcissistic behaviour? This sheer hypocrisy is a sign that many people of the left, have and still are, being duped.

Their stupidity knows no bounds. Ever since the LGBT movement came to prominence, they have sought to raise awareness of any social inequality. Legalised gay marriage is one thing, but for new born children to have their sex "nominated" according to their parents' wishes is ludicrous. A penis present on a newborn at birth, indicates a boy and a vagina signals a female. End of discussion for normal folk!

But no, the left need to play gender politics. You can be what your parents want you to be at birth. Yep! boys can legally be raised as girls! What is scarier is that parts of Australia under lefty control have passed this into law. Social engineering should not be tolerated. That's sure to be a winner for the sound mental health of these future teenagers. Not!

The LGBT crowd want all personal information forms to do away with the first question of "male or female?" They instead, suggest a myriad of alternatives such as "male, female, bisexual, transgender." Purely crazy stuff. This serves to create a "sexual dysphoria" in our impressionable youth, as people are given the freedom to create a new identity for themselves.

While our education standards slip, the lefties are more concerned about our primary-school children having a greater understanding of homosexuality and gender queerness. This is really going to help them catch up in their numeracy and literacy skills! No wonder the quality of our school kids' education has never been poorer. Where is the emphasis on restructuring the curriculum to improve literacy and numeracy?

Transgender athletes have been given permission to compete at the highest levels of sport. Olympic medals have been won in women's running events, where athletes born as men are allowed to compete as women. Even after genital reassignment, higher residual testosterone levels give these transgender athletes a height, weight, and strength advantage. In seeking equality for an individual or minority, ruling sports administrators have gone woke and undermined fairness for the majority. Once again, a hypocritical outcome arising from wokeness. To stand up against this, is to be vilified by the left, and condemned as sexist or even just plain racist.

Male or female categorisation is the basis for jails, public amenity blocks, or sports teams. It's not that difficult. But the left is saying you are not male or female, but rather what you identify yourself as. So yes, the left is implying that little Johnny can go and register for the under seven girls' nippers at his local surf club. Little Johnny and his woke parents may selfishly feel that is in his best interests. But what of the other fifty young girls and their families, that are horrified at the prospect of a little boy beating all the girls in their little races. And as for an exposed penis in the female amenities block…? The legalised same-sex marriage referendum result "opened the gate and the horse has bolted."

In releasing a minority few from suppression of their feelings and beliefs, the LGBT crowd have "raised the ire" of large sections of the community. You are now free to use the male or female amenities block depending on how you identify yourself. They are creating a haven for paedophiles and sexual perverts to "prey on the vulnerable" in public toilet blocks. More madness from the left.

The Greens and all socialists want to placate any group that feels persecuted. The indigenous are also a worthy target of their policies. Lefties wish to move Australia day, just because it offends the Aboriginal community. Christmas and Christmas decorations have been banned in some areas, because some religious groups and ethnic minorities may take offense. Easter is another problem, as some do not want any celebration of the death and resurrection of Christ.

In recent times, the activists have even taken to protesting outside jails, in order to have Aboriginals released from custody. They ignore the fact that their higher rates of incarceration are because of their greater propensity to break the law, and not their skin colour or unfair treatment by the police.

If you don't want to stand and sing the national anthem at school, well that's ok too. The lefties tell the teachers and principals that the kids have rights, and you cannot force them to do something against their will or belief. So much for instilling respect and discipline. School principals have even lost their jobs, for suspending and expelling students with poor discipline records.

Socialist lefties thrive on the power that comes with implementing change, and "to hell with the consequences." Their intent is to virtue signal. What ever happened to opposition political parties offering different economic perspectives that can improve whole economies and nations?

The progressives only offer "tokenistic" measures that do not help society progress. This does nothing to fix inequalities. It only serves to rile the moderate centre and those of the right. The left has a history of financial ineptitude. When they were last in power, they were more moderate in trying to at least "placate" the sensible centre. But by being in opposition, recent events have radicalised them. Worse still, they are becoming more brazen in their attacks on capitalism and those of the right, as society seems unwilling to stand up to them.

An example of mistakes being made in the past but being unnecessarily repeated, is readily apparent when looking at foreign aid expenditure by First World governments.

Economic growth has generated enough revenue for governments to be able to afford generous foreign aid, which is then distributed to Third World countries. These poorer nations often have high levels of poverty and starvation. Unfortunately, they are also often adversely affected by weather extremes such as droughts, which accentuate their famines.

History has shown that foreign aid distributed in the form of money, quickly disappears at the hands of corrupt government officials. There is little benefit that actually filters down and reaches the needy population. It is wiser, to offer inventory such as machinery, training, housing supplies, and even food supplies, in lieu of cold, hard cash.

This foreign aid money is better spent subsidising local manufacturing and the production of necessary supplies, and then exporting the products to the needy. This simultaneously, further boosts local economic growth and prevents foreign monetary aid disappearing into the pockets of corrupt foreign governments. "More bang for your buck."

It seems that this lesson has not been learnt. Marginalised minority groups such as the Aboriginal community, have been generously supported by the Australian taxpayer. But despite the vast expenditure, the Aboriginal community is still afflicted by social issues of lower educational standard, higher poverty levels, greater propensity to be involved in crime, and lower life expectancy. Two things to note on this issue.

Firstly, money is not the answer. Despite the massive expense over the years, nearly all policies have failed to deliver a better outcome for many of Australia's indigenous community. It is time to re-educate the parents and elders of the Aborigines about the importance of discipline in raising their children. There's that "unsexy" word again.

Another way to view this, is to imagine a homeless person coming up to you and asking for "two-dollars for a cup of coffee." The homeless person would willingly take two-dollars off you, but would tell you "bugger off," if you offered to buy them a cup of coffee. Its all about the money.

Secondly, the recent socialist cries that "Black Lives Matter," after one death in custody of an arrested person of black skin, highlights the hypocrisy of the left. What about the thousands of abuse cases inflicted on young Aborigines by their own parents and minders? Aborigines cry "racism," yet they are ignorant of their treatment of their own. "People in glass houses shouldn't throw stones." Thousands of Aborigines protested about black deaths in custody, but where are their voices complaining about Aboriginal infant mortality rates?

Whilst the BLM protests were going on around the world, in Townsville, Australia, a fourteen-year-old Aboriginal boy stole a car, picked up his Aboriginal friends and went on a break-and-enter spree over the weekend. When spotted by police, the unlicensed juvenile sped off at high speed with his mates as passengers. Being unlicensed, he lost control of the car, crashed into a tree and killed his three young friends. The story barely made the news and there was no reporting about the Aboriginal identity of the youths. This was an epic tragedy that no one wanted to talk about. Again, the hypocrisy knows no bounds, as the facts in this incident, do not support the narrative of the left.

The old "stolen generation" argument was also hijacked by the socialists. Years ago, a few young Aboriginal children were removed from their families, not because of racism, but for their own safety. Yet the truth has been distorted to fit today's narrative. "White man" was at fault here, as the Aboriginal representatives seek reparations and compensation to be forwarded to those affected. It's all about the money.

Yes, our Aboriginal friends are crying out for more equality. Well, maybe we should give them what they want. The government should remove free and subsidized education for indigenous aboriginals. Afterall, this is clearly racist against the "white man." Likewise, the government should remove subsidized housing from Aboriginals. Afterall, many do not appreciate what they have been given. Many have their hands out all the time and yet, are quick to "stab the white fella in the back."

Many Aborigines now refer to us Australian settlers as "invaders," and resent the fact that they have been "colonised." They detest Australia Day and consider it to be "invasion day." Personally, I think they should count themselves as lucky. History has shown that Australia would not have remained undiscovered for much longer. The Aboriginals should "thank their lucky stars" that they were not "invaded" by the Chinese. In that case, their plight might have been worse than that of the Uyghurs and other minority Muslim groups, who are treated "inhumanely" in mainland China.

Hypocritical again, to blame the "white man" for the fact that many Aboriginal youths are abused by their parents and elders. Sad too, that Aboriginal kids as young as three years old, are carrying sexually transmitted diseases such as syphilis and gonorrhoea. As per usual, the socialists overlook the facts. Clear evidence that they are not really interested in the welfare of all individuals. They are "trojan horse jockeys," whose only goal is to be in power.

In America, leftist attempts to remove Donald Trump from Presidency saw them attack his character based on his reputed treatment of women. Women's advocate groups such as "Me Too," denounced his alleged previous behaviour, and allowed the Democrats to weaponize sexual abuse claims against the President.

This was accentuated a year later, when the President decided to appoint Justice Brett Kavanaugh to the Supreme Court. The left "dug up dirt" on this man from thirty-odd years prior, in order to denounce his character, and to have his appointment nullified. They used unsubstantiated lies, to support the case of a supposed victim of sexual abuse, allegedly carried out by Mr Kavanaugh. They perpetuated a lie, to fight their objection of having a right-leaning judge, appointed to the Supreme Court. The lying though, was soon to be superseded by the blatant hypocrisy of the left.

In trying to denigrate Mr Kavanaugh, "believe all women" became the catchcry, and slogan for all supporters and media of the left. But when the Democrat (left) nominee for the upcoming 2020 Presidential election, Joe Biden was accused of a similar sexual assault, the silence was deafening. Oh, the hypocrisy! The media did not report the claims, and even went as far as to discredit the claimant, Tara Reade. Media political allegiances have been drawn in the sand. This is dangerous for society as a whole. Another example of that duality prevalent in society today!

The greatest hypocrisy has revealed itself in the "Black Lives Matter" protests around the world. One little incident in Minneapolis, and all of a sudden "everyone is tarred with the same brush." This quickly descended into a protest at racism. Not only that, the cry of Black Lives Matter was loudest during the outbreak of covid-19. Given that social distancing laws were broken, clearly nobody was concerned about transmission of the highly contagious virus. It seemed that nobody else's lives mattered.

By definition, racism refers to prejudice or antagonism directed against persons or people, on the basis of belonging to a particular racial or ethnic group. It does not assert moral superiority of one race over another. While the BLM protestors feel aggrieved at the suppression of black people, the vast majority of white people are not racist. Yet they are vilified and denounced as racist, purely because they ignore the protests. Again "people in glass houses should not throw stones." It is the BLM protestors who often appear racist and who are quick to judge alternate opinions as racist. This is a cynical stance and is drawing condemnation from peaceful, law-abiding folk.

This "reverse racism" is now another tool currently being used by the left to destabilize Western society. It is why the anarchists of antifa deface and destroy, statues and monuments of our founders. Erase history and then all traces of yesteryear slavery disappear. But their hatred of the system that has created so much prosperity, knows no bounds. They will not rest until capitalism is destroyed.

Hence the need to understand their cries of "defund the police." Deep down, the leftists are really after power and control. They have manipulated a large proportion of the media to control thoughts and minds with leftist propaganda. As we have seen, wealth accumulated through capitalism has to be preserved and enhanced, for future generations to benefit from a strong national defence and sufficient law and order resources.

Locally, a strong law and order system is pivotal to preventing violence and to keep the peace. Some elected lefty leaders are now even calling for police forces to be abolished altogether. As we have seen in Seattle, having no law and order does nothing for social cohesion and personal safety. Rather it is just another mechanism, through which the socialists wish to attain power, by destabilizing the ruling governments.

Nigel Farage of Brexit fame summed it up best. He was recently in Australia when on a guest-speaking tour down under. While he was in Sydney, he was thrown a question from the floor. A wise young gentleman embarking on a career in the corporate world, asked "what was the best way to make it to the top of a company, if you had a strong opinion, and you had a political persuasion to the right?"

Without hesitation, Mr Farage quipped "I suggest you keep your mouth shut or better still, open your own company." Subtle and succinct, but certainly right on the money. The rising intolerance of everything by the left, is giving rise to the trend of people "keeping their thoughts and opinions to themselves." Large sections of the community are being intimidated into submission. This has made things tough for pollsters trying to predict election results.

Despite maintaining silence or discretion regarding your views and opinions, pollsters still seek to ascertain what the population is thinking as a whole. "Fake polls" are now often used to support an agenda. Questions can often be asked of respondents in a "subjective manner" in order to acquire a favoured outcome. Even the pollsters are not immune from being biased. This is seen in their "targeting" of selective audiences to try to conjure a preconceived, preferred result for their polls. The fake poll results are then reported by the fake news merchants, to convince you to vote in the manner they prefer. Known alternatively as "coercion."

In the recent elections in Australia, America, and the United Kingdom, the pre-election polls got the results horribly wrong. In Australia, so sure was one sports betting agency of a Labor victory (based on pre-election polling trends), that they decided to pay out on a Labor victory twenty-four hours before the election. Punters who backed Labor, were remunerated with their winnings prior to the election. Twenty-four hours later, and the Liberals had retained government in an astounding victory. What a bunch of idiots!

Thankfully, what this demonstrated to the whole world, was that despite the noise, exuberance, and blatant aggression of the Labor left, the quiet Australian's are not "buying into" this socialism. The resultant post-election disbelief from the left, is not unlike the Trump Derangement Syndrome of America. Frustrated at their inability to gain office and the power that comes with it, there are now factional forces seeking to undermine leaders, by moving the Labor party to the far-left to embrace complete socialism.

This phenomenon may also explain why Facebook and Twitter are regarded as the "domain of the socialists." Contributions are predominantly by the woke, feel-good lefties. Anyone who objects is often subjected to ridicule, criticism, and vilification.

Common sense, among inhabitants of the West, is not in total short supply, thankfully. American Republican congress members are starting to call out the "heavy bias towards the left" of the operators of Google, Apple, Amazon, Twitter, and Facebook. Given that they monopolize their respective media platforms, they have been free to control the social narrative, edit online material to their own discretion, fill staff positions with progressives only, and pay minimal taxes. Their behaviour can influence election results, far more easily than any Russian or Ukrainian "supposedly" can.

These tech giants from Silicon Valley are overplaying their hand. They have the ability to enhance the cyber-warfare capabilities of the military. Why is it, that they have opted to not involve themselves with the United States military, and yet are eager to assist the Chinese in their warfare capabilities? No wonder TikTok, operated by Chinese interests, took off as quick as it did. The power of the "yuan" is too much for the technocrats to resist.

To hell with the private data of Western citizens, when there is a dollar to be made off the Chinese. America and other Western nations are on the verge of being sold out from within; … by their own countrymen! What is it with greed? Remember our lessons from before? About the importance of communications in maintaining economic and military strength.

Donald Trump is correct to be wary of the significance of social media influencing outcomes of future elections. A tool for propaganda, their subliminal messaging has recently given way to rampant bias towards the left.

Even google has been hi-jacked by the left. The internet derives its speed and strength from "key word" engine drive algorithms. Tech-savvy advertising personnel and Information Technology (IT) specialists, are able to influence what you read first, by biased algorithm programming. For example, a google search of Donald Trump will see the "leading" related, listed web articles displayed, all favour the left. The user is subjected to negative articles first, all detrimental to the perception of Donald Trump and the Republicans. Again, we need to educate our future voters about this strategy.

In June 2020, Donald Trump held a pre-election rally on behalf of the Republicans. It was touted as a massive sell out, with over one million folk registering for tickets to the rally. Alas, only 6,500 turned up in a stadium that seats 19,000. It is alleged that "Instagram" ran a campaign for its young followers to register for tickets and then not turn up. It obviously worked. But what does this mean for future elections?

Can mail votes or ballots be corrupted by social mediums such as Facebook and Instagram? In the future, given that the left just disregards the truth and ignore the facts, can the vote counters at polling booths be trusted to report accurate counts?

Our young, impressionable, future voters need to objectively question what they are seeing, hearing, and reading, and also learn to recognise the truth and bias in reporting, for themselves. Certain television channels, newspapers, plus social media platforms such as Facebook and Twitter, are all biased towards the left. This should be kept in mind when viewing them. These can be fine to share photos and thoughts with family and friends, but they become dangerous when the truth is disregarded and the facts are ignored.

The bias and favouritism engulfing the left has important implications for society. For governments to pass new laws, a lack of bipartisanship at a federal level, can see some legislation passed to the Supreme Court for determination of fairness and validity.

Unfortunately, a left or right bias in elected Supreme Court Judges, can influence the ability to govern with strength and conviction, by passing or rejecting these motions. It is well known that Republicans (right) in America, need a majority of supportive Judges at Supreme Court level, just to have their proposed legislation changes ratified. The same thing is now happening in Australia and other leading Western nations.

It has been shown, that the left has infiltrated every level of society, and have thrown their support behind any group treated unfairly. They are creating a revolution for disaffected minorities. Previous left-leaning political parties, once proud and enjoying respect from the sensible centre, have lost their soul, in siding with the greens and socialists in order to boost their voting base. This is playing out before a worldwide audience, like never before, due to extensive media coverage.

Just like lefty activism is dominating media headlines, the silence of the right is now "deafening." A lot of ordinary folk are dismayed at the unrest in society. You cannot just see and hear it in the media or on the streets. "You can feel it!" The time for complacency has passed. Capitalism and the freedom that it nurtures, if it is to be preserved, has to be fought for, and defended like never before.

This chapter has been so easy to write, and yet so hard to restrict to one common thread or topic. Notice how every issue has been politicized and weaponized in the same manner. Just as globalisation has turned the countries of the world into one tiny village, the battle between left and right, has overwhelmed everything and everyone in society. Separate issues are intrinsically interwoven due to common battle lines of left or right.

Virtually everything can be explained, not by science or facts, but by who is telling the story. The conservatives or the progressives are putting forward two separate views on everything. "God help us" if we ever confront a "seriously" deadly virus or an invading enemy. You won't know what to believe. Again, more duality which is slowly tearing society apart. This battle is reducing overall quality of life, as people are mentally, at their "wit's end."

9.4 Wokeness, the Achilles heel of the socialists

There is no doubt, that those of the left, have derived their strength by taking up the wokeness mantle. They have grown a voice, through biased leftist media outlets and the control of social media platforms by left-leaning technocrats. They have garnered the support of the disillusioned, the disaffected, and the under-privileged.

They appeal to anyone who feels disparaged or offended in any way. They even take pity on the miscreants of society and invite them into their "socialist church." But they forget and deliberately ignore one very important fact. Socialism has not succeeded anywhere. Ever! It does not have a strong base or foundation upon which to build. Socialism also takes time and multiple generations, in order to become a new way of life. It requires inter-generational adoption of the philosophy.

While it is a loud, aggressive movement, it does not afford its citizens, a means to generate wealth in the long run. It only piles misery and suffering on its followers. The socialist elite seek to rule. They crave the power, currently enjoyed by capitalist Western nations which are governed by conservatives throughout the world.

The use of wokeness to destroy the West from within, will hopefully be a passing fad, just like many that have gone before. The covid-19 pandemic seems to have opened people's eyes once more, to the real issues confronting mankind. Woke issues are being dramatized by the left, while the conservatives quietly ignore this intrusion into their life, by simply going about their business of making money and getting on with life.

The obsession with this new cancel culture, may give the keyboard warriors perceived power, but is does nothing to enhance their wealth. It is amazing to see, how the woke warriors have become empowered, when they facelessly, seek to encourage the boycott of goods and services provided by conservative individuals and companies. This cancel culture is creating a false sense of power for these unfortunate souls. I can only assume that they have fallen into the trap of being "tall poppies." But their voice is based on nothing. They are not offering "anything" to replace what they want destroyed.

The greatest example of the pathetic wokeness, must surely be Meghan Markle. This attractive young lady, was the envy of the female world, when she captured the heart of Prince Harry. The most eligible bachelor of the British Royal family, Harry had the world at his feet, and was to be the shining light of the royal family, after the death of his mother Princess Diana.

Young Meghan waltzed into Buckingham Palace, married Prince Harry in a lavish ceremony watched worldwide by millions, and then decided that she hates all the royal commitments and scrutiny. How dare she complain of the riches lavished upon her. Ungrateful and selfish to say the least.

Not content with royal life, she whisked him out of the country, and dragged him away from all his "lad" and military force commitments. Having lost their royal entitlements, they now take up the fight for the woke brigade to retain popularity. For one who detested being in the spotlight, Meghan is perhaps the greatest "hypocrite" of all time. She is now "Princess Woke" and is encouraging saturation coverage of all things woke in the media.

As for Harry? He has gone from being a "good bloke" to being a "good woke." Son, you have married a shocker! That thing on the top of your head, is not a receding hairline. It is a massive thumbprint. You are so under the thumb, it is embarrassing. She is "wearing the pants" now, my friend! That being the case, the United Kingdom dodged a bullet, in avoiding having such a weak man possibly becoming King one day.

Wokeness even instils weakness into normal civilian life. Just look at socialist efforts to take competition out of our young, in their junior sporting contests. Rather than have winners or losers, our young will never learn the nature of combat and conflict, as they will be conditioned to participate, rather than win or lose in sporting contests. Pride, passion, and the "will to win," are currently being discouraged and eroded by the elitist lefties, who wish to have equality for all. "It's not whether you win or lose, it's how you play the game." I am sure those sentiments, were traditionally echoed by the "losers" in days gone by.

Even the individual pursuit of academic excellence, is being constrained, as the left seeks to ensure everyone achieves a minimum standard of education, rather than encouraging high achievers to maximise their potential. They wish for equality, to the point that they force companies to employ on gender quota, rather than ability.

Wokeness is even exerted on lending institutions, to force them not to invest in industries such as mining, which can be harmful to the environment. Common sense will tell you that if you do not "grow the pie," there is less for everyone. The socialists are "planning to fail" in their indoctrination of society. Yes, our friends from the left are "a few cents short of the dollar," and certainly not "the sharpest tool in the shed." Therein, lies their weakness. "if it isn't broken, then don't fix it!"

Socialism at first, is often faceless and can appear to be rudderless, as it "bubbles away on the surface." But, "scratch the surface and look a little deeper." There is "the old chestnut" of that "lust for power" lurking just below the surface, and being exhibited by an elitist few.

Leading progressive politicians, the power-seeking, lefty-aligned media, and the social media technocrats, are merely trying to subvert minds through wokeness, to gain ascendancy at election time. They care not for the welfare of the masses. They seek to control them by giving them a voice and then ignoring them, once they have the power or are in charge. As, with all narcissists, there is no discipline, just a desire to be on top, through vilification and intimidation of opponents.

This is no economic basis, for the ongoing development of an ordered, successful democratic society offered by the progressives. Just the incessant denunciation of all opposing views. Sound familiar?

Recognise the sheer hypocrisy of the leftists, as a sign of their deceit and insincere motives. One only has to look at the agitators of the global warming hoax. The elites have gotten rich, out of peddling fake news about catastrophic heating of the earth and rising sea levels.

The socialist elite are so concerned about this, that they purchase the most expensive water-side mansions possible. Can you "smell the rat?" "It is only a rort, if you are not in on it." While many get sucked in, thankfully, Western society still does, have enough collective intelligence, and the ability to rationalise, thereby seeing through the veneer that is socialism.

Indeed, the Chinese Communist Party while being an emerging global threat, is still plagued with dissatisfaction by the many oppressed inhabitants within the nation. While the West is wise to confront the Communist China, the application of maximum economic pressure on the regime through trade tariffs, should ultimately, see the CCP turn on itself. The CCP will be met at borders if need be, but ultimately it will be defeated from within, by natural socio-economic forces. Or a self-inflicted virus maybe!

At the end of the day, history has shown that just as socialism is about to achieve its "utopia," it slides into communism. Once totalitarian control of the people is reached, natural forces of human nature give rise to rebellion against the authoritative control over the people. It is in essence, a self-defeating philosophy. A common sense means of wealth redistribution, that has been hijacked by leftist extremists, who seek power, by preaching the need to uphold morality through equality. But once there is no wealth left to plunder, growing poverty and economic hardship within, sow the seeds of change.

9.5 Every cloud has a silver lining

The saving grace for us all is that historically, revolutions are doomed to fail. Political revolutions seek not only to establish a new political system, but transform an entire society. However, such sweeping transformations of a society, can take several generations to bring about complete reform.

By that time, factional infighting among those seeking to rebel, often snuffs out the revolution. Afterall, is was noted socialist Vladimir Lenin who wrote "that the goal of socialism is communism." Socialism still creates its own elite, who have their own personal battles to be the most powerful. Even then, to make it to the top, you need to have a significant armed force behind you. This force is accompanied by propaganda to reach the hearts and minds of the people. Creating an army of followers, strengthens the revolutionary push for power.

Until recent years, Western democracies have enjoyed stable governments, that occasionally alternated in left and right political persuasion. Today, the growing inequalities and massive population pressures have turned up the heat on political parties. Impatience has grown among those not getting their share of the pie in the fashion they wish. We are witnessing natural, cyclical, socioeconomic forces.

Desperation for power is reflected in the ignorance of the truth and facts. Just look at the lies and untruths of today's lefties. Does Western society have the stomach today, to confront socialism like it has in the past? History is repeating itself, especially when you compare social uprisings of the past, such as that of Lenin in Russia between 1917-1924. Lenin had implemented mass socialism, but the promises of a better society, were far removed from the reality that ensued. Poverty and racial tensions abounded, as Russia sought to retain control of neighbouring states.

At the same time, communism was also on the rise with Germany, Italy, Japan, and North Korea forming the Axis powers, but as we have seen, this was defeated in World War Two. As the left wishes to erase history, it is imperative that these lessons are not lost.

It is vital for law and order to be maintained, and to not give in to anarchy, like that witnessed at Chaz, Seattle. With time, rebellions often fail as infighting among minorities sees them "shoot themselves in the foot." The Democrats in America are fighting among themselves on which way to get elected. The quiet Americans, are hopefully, surveying the damage on display in all lefty governed states. Maybe the lefty media, and their efforts to create hatred and division, in their bias, will turn people totally against the left. The next American election will "make or break" this economic super power. We know what happens if America sneezes!

Just as we had the back of the Liberals, the Republicans, and the Conservatives, at the ballot box, our elected governments need to "grow a back-bone" and stand up for us against the socialist movement. Know that political correctness and wokeness are tools of the left, that have been allowed to permeate society. Ironically, they sow the seeds of division.

"Actions speak louder than words." So true, as virtue signalling is easily done, but has rarely led to successful policy implementation. Knowing this and having witnessed recent world events, the time is ripe like never before, to stand up to the unrest at our doorstep.

Those of the right, need to have courage to enter politics, despite persecution from the left. Capitalism requires strong-willed orators and defenders to ensure it prevails. People not afraid to denounce the ramblings of the left, as nothing more than wishful thinking. To cave in to the woke brigade from the left, is to surrender all that your country stands for.

Our heroic Anzac soldiers fought and died for the very blanket of freedom under which we live. Of course, this is forgotten in the attempted erasure of our history by the lefties and socialism. Fortunately, the 2020 pandemic has renewed the vigour in the fight to preserve nationalism.

It has temporarily subdued leftist calls for open borders thankfully. It has been a time of re-evaluating what is really important. For instance, for local economies to recover from the pandemic, the local unemployed should be given first priority in seeking work opportunities. The days of relying on immigrants to fill skill and worker shortages are for the time being, gone. The left won't be happy, but nations now have to look after their own first.

The Pandemic, while taking many lives, may also serve to save us from the growing threat of communist China. The totalitarian behaviour of the Chinese Communist Party had previously been ignored. Our preoccupation with the left-right battle from within, saw us "take our eyes off the ball." It is hoped that socialism can be defeated, and the West can remain a pillar of economic strength. Afterall, history has shown, that communism has and must be defeated, for freedom and democracy to exist.

To coin a phrase, the old Aussie vernacular has never been more apt. "She'll be right." Seems that things are ok if they stay this way. But it pays to not be complacent. While the left need to re-analyse their recent actions and come back to the sensible centre, the whole world needs to prepare to confront the greater threat of communist China.

The "saving grace" for those supporters of capitalism, is that to date, to combat the emergence of the radical left, no one has yet to "lift a finger." The vast majority of quiet folk truly understand the importance of law and order. They know the need to promote economic growth. "The proof is in the pudding." When "push comes to shove," they know how to repel the advances of socialism. Afterall, "the pen is mightier than the sword."

Simple sayings that sum up a battle that has been waged for years. And, as with all socialist uprisings, there has only ever been one outcome. Remember too, that we pointed out that you never interrupt the enemy when he is making a mistake. Let's hope this continues to be the case.

Capitalism has provided a platform of freedom, where man has the opportunity to go seek his fortune without impediments. To "take the road less travelled," is to discover new things and enjoy new experiences. Socialist lefties have chosen to take the well-trodden path, where there is nothing worthy to be found, as others have gone before.

Afterall, isn't the definition of insanity "to do the same thing over and over, and expect a different outcome?" It certainly explains all that we see and know about socialism. Socialists are in denial of this salient point.

The left has become more and more unhinged, and yet have not accomplished anything, except to divide society. They have created racism out of something that wasn't there (for the main part), just to attract supporters. One cannot eat a "redskin" lolly anymore because you might offend someone. They are "chasing after shadows." Today, they object to a simple piano. Is it because the white keys are bigger than the black keys?

The board game "chess" is under attack because of black and white pieces, where white gets to go first. The famous American Football team, the Washington Redskins now have to change their name and all marketing paraphernalia because their name is offensive. Really? That they stoop so low is a sign of their desperation. Coon cheese has had to change its name, even though it was named after its founder; all because the name may offend people of Aboriginal decent. All these measures are doing nothing to create jobs, generate dollars, or feed the masses.

The socialist movement has been driven by elites and activist groups. George Soros, a supporter of progressive governments, has donated tens of billions of dollars to socialist causes. Is this multi-billionaire trying to play the markets by upsetting economies? Activist groups such as "getup," "extinction rebellion," and "me too," may have different fronts, but each has a common goal. To destroy capitalism. It "begs the question" … are they secretly being funded by the Chinese Communist Party?

History has shown that socialism fails. Have the last few years demonstrated the fact that "a watched pot never boils." Are we watching socialism eat itself up, before it can even complete its attempted revolution? The left seems to be "clutching at straws" so much, that even current leaders of left political parties are conspicuous in their absence. Are they embarrassed, or do they realise that "they are flogging a dead horse?"

It is poignant to note too, that the leftie elites are not afraid of the socialist mob that is going after capitalism. Afterall, they are in fact in control of the mob. Their tools of choice are the media and social platforms. Their goals are abundantly clear. But they remain ignorant of history, and seek to deny you and your children, the chance to learn about it.

Note too, the sheer arrogance of the "so-called" elites. The Jeffrey Epstein death reveals a lot about the power and corruption at the top of the tree. Child sex rings, paedophilia, and mass corruption, among the elites, are only now starting to play out. Notice how celebrities and certain prominent members of Hollywood are starting to turn on each other, whilst looking down on the rest of society. Consumed by power, they have all done very little to further the cause of ordinary man (humankind). Time to wake up and "smell the roses."

Our early pioneers forged empires, something the lefties conveniently ignore, as they try to erase history. "You will never cross the ocean, if you are afraid to lose sight of the shore." It pays to remember this. The strength of our early pioneers, is needed now in our elected leaders and prominent members of society, as they stand up to protect us from the dangers of socialism. Support also has to be forth-coming for our police, to quell growing unrest on our streets.

Our leaders have to restore the fundamentals back into our education system. History, science, the arts, and literature, are noble subjects. They have to somehow, be inter-twined with the tendency to now offer subjects that afford the greatest employment opportunities. Cyclical left and right-leaning governments, have left the teaching fraternity intact. They are free to deliver education with any twist they so desire, and without proper intervention from above. It's time for an education overhaul.

Our leaders cannot allow the media to be solely owned by right or left-leaning propaganda merchants. Objectivity in reporting of news should be encouraged. Social platforms should be regulated, to prevent bias from one political persuasion or the other.

Also, of note here, is that red tape, government regulations, higher taxes, and wokeness, have all strangled the life out of us all. We are being stifled by an "Orwellian" control over our behaviour, our thoughts, our words, and our actions. Surveillance and scrutiny of our every move, has fatigued us like never before. Maybe the socialists are onto something, in wanting to break free and just "catch a breath."

But no, the reality is, that their movement is a drive for power, hidden in the ultimate trojan horse, "morality." Therein, lies the danger. They suggest nothing, in terms of policy, that can improve overall wealth for all. They merely seek to destroy the wealth and freedom of the privileged. They have failed in their own education and career ambitions. As such, they seek to bring down those who have excelled. They are dragging society down, to the level of the lowest common denominator. That's right, they want us all to be equally poor. That makes for a better society according to their ridiculous ideology.

Everything is in your face, or at least in the palm of your hand so it seems. Those of the right are doing their best to make ends meet and keep up. Those who rationalise the intrusion of lefty propaganda, soldier on regardless. Many of the lefties, have seemingly dropped out of the race, and become non-contributors or dismayed at the fact they don't get to "share in the spoils." When confronted with adversity, they want to pursue the path of least resistance.

Whether it be free education, free healthcare, public housing, rental assistance, unemployment benefits, subsidies for this and that, the pension, or good old government stimulus payments, there are too many with their hands out. With massive debt levels already, nations and economies are at breaking point. Hence the "last throw of the dice" for the socialists. They want higher taxes for those left working, to fuel their insatiable appetite for free money. Instead of "rolling up their sleeves," they denigrate those who do, and opt instead, for the easy path. The path to oblivion.

And so, the battle wages on. At the end of the day, regardless of what you have, life as we know it, will change forever without law and order. The lessons have been learnt. Our leaders have to stand up for capitalism, and the rest of us mere mortals have to ensure we know the difference between left and right. It has never been more important, to instil knowledge of political differences, into our children and young adults. If we don't, you can "bet your bottom dollar" that without capitalism, we will be fighting the Chinese in years to come with "sticks and stones."

9.6 All is not lost

Learning. Such a simple philosophy. It is a capability within us all. It does not discriminate, divide or segregate society. We all seek a life full of happiness, wealth, good health, and wonderful experiences. Regardless of your religion, skin colour, culture or economic status, we are all raised by our parents, with a common goal. Food and warmth in abundance, and hopefully an education and upbringing to prepare us for adult life. "We are masters of our own destiny."

Just look at our obsession with words. They convey meaning and information, but they also serve to protect, define, and ultimately, determine. Media publications, academic papers, contracts, medical reports, lawsuits, infringement notices, and company by-laws, are all powerful tools influencing behaviour. We live in an ordered society, where there is a massive flow of dollars, dependent on what is "written" and "spoken."

Add technology to the mix, and we become even more transfixed by words and language. We have become more averse to sending a text message or email, rather than picking up the phone to have a verbal conversation. Somehow, they are perceived to be faster, even though they are in fact, a slower means of conveying information. Whether they be spoken or written, our words can also come back to haunt us. Just ask Joe Biden.

Modern language is now littered with words that make no sense, but which speed things up, such is our appetite for information. Abbreviations, slang, and emojis, being used in lieu of words, is the new norm. Are we losing their sense of meaning and true impetus in the process? We cannot afford to lose the art of conversation. When we can speak up without fear, then we can also truly rationalise, argue, defend, criticize, and question, what is being preached to us under the "pretext" of being better for us.

What is written and sent via service providers, has become conclusive proof in courts of law, resulting in some people being punished for their indiscretions. Our language is getting us into trouble all of a sudden. We seem to have taken our knowledge on this matter for granted. Just like we have with the rise of socialism.

The leftie socialists have "in their unfounded wisdom," decided to use the strength of the Western nations and turn it into a weakness. They have politicised and weaponised language. What was once a means of mandating legislation, a method of communication, a tool for learning, and a guide to civil obedience, has been undermined. Even science, which is the study of the relationship between cause and effect, has been compromised, as words can be corruptly or unethically used to support or deny certain narratives.

Language is perhaps the greatest tool in the socialist arsenal. Words are now used to exaggerate inequalities or differences that are often non-existent. Political leaders now use words, rather than policies, to persuade voters to elect them. Protesters, with catchy slogans plastered all over banners, are testimony to the power of language.

The problem with all this, is that lies are allowed to be perpetuated. They are printed, published, and repeatedly told, on many social platforms and television networks. When this happens, lies can become the truth. At this point, words lose their meaning and the value of language is diminished. Only a few brave media commentators are calling out this behaviour. Laws need to be reviewed and adjusted to eradicate this phenomenon. False advertising is one thing, but fake news should be punishable by law, with heavy fines or loss of licenses, for any individual or entity that propagates mis-truths.

Advertisers bombard us with marketing phrases to sell products. Whenever we buy a product or sign a contract, we are urged to "check the fine print." But how often do we scrutinize what we hear? We need to recognise, the ulterior motive of the source of information, and know the bigger picture like never before. Check out the "click bait" on your "iPhone" trying to get your attention. It is as though we are mesmerized by the constant bombardment of information. Not unlike a rabbit trying to cross the road at night, blinded by the headlights of an oncoming vehicle! But it is the subliminal messaging that is the real danger.

It pays to understand the motives of the authors of what you read. Journalists are out of a job, if they cannot report stories that sell newspapers. Media publishers and broadcasters, in all their many forms, rely on advertising and subscriptions to make a profit. Politicians attract votes by alerting constituents to their intended policies. Notice how everything is based upon the pursuit of money. With the wealth, is where the power resides.

Today, who controls the words, controls the future. The source of what you see or hear, is of the utmost importance. The left has resorted to deception, fear-mongering, and vilification, through language and aggressive behaviour. They are exaggerating and twisting words to support their narrative. Certain broadcasters are conditioning society to hear what they want us to hear. We are being scared into believing the socialist narrative.

Whether it be bushfire headlines, the boxing day tsunami, climate change, covid-19, earthquakes, plane crashes, political upheavals or social issues, the "words" used in headlines, are manipulated to catastrophize the story. The more pronounced the issue or the greater the magnitude of the event, the more the dollars flow. Remember that deadly sin "greed."

The socialist movement does not care for the individual. They merely crave power and money. The Marxists (extreme left progressives) are the trojan horse jockeys riding any pertinent issue to further their cause. They are duping the gullible, less educated, unknowing, and non-contributors of society, into supporting their cause. As we have seen, they are solely focused on destroying capitalist nations. As they fumble about in general elections, they seek to destabilize society, which in turn, will hit us all "in the hip pocket."

So, is socialism doomed? Is this current uprising an example of socialism turning on itself? The way the BLM protests have been infiltrated by anarchists, will soon see more of the wise lefties abandon voting for progressive political parties. All revolutions in history have failed, as the socialists turn on themselves. The fact that socialists want to remove law and order says it all.

We have seen that the anarchists are only capable of "running around like headless chooks!" I will probably get in trouble for saying that, but they are doing nothing which indicates they are capable of governing an ordered society, in a fiscally and democratically responsible manner. Let us pray that this continues to be the case.

One thing is for sure, education is the future. Not socialism. We owe it to our children to teach them about the difference between left and right. We just cannot trust the teachers of today to do this. The Teacher Unions that now run our education systems, have become ever more powerful, and are almost militant in nature. It is hard for an individual teacher to deliver subject content objectively. The teachers who try to do this are "swimming against the tide."

Currently, at the time of writing, schools in America in lefty states, are remaining closed in response to the pandemic, even though the covid-19 virus does not adversely affect the young. The teachers are forgoing the educational wellbeing of their students, in preference for political point-scoring against the sitting United States President. Obviously, more evidence that education has succumbed to politization too. Again, it is the left or progressives who are after power, rather than the optimal outcome for students. This is creating further duality in society, as private education and greater parental input, now afford our young greater educational opportunities. Indeed, Donald Trump is even considering withdrawing funding for schools that elect to not reopen.

Until our Australian education curriculum is completely overhauled, progressive indoctrination of our nation's children will continue. Our sliding down the education rankings, is because the teaching of mathematics and English has, "taken a backseat," and been surpassed by an emphasis on emotional wellbeing, inclusivity, and gender studies. Teachers are now starting to infringe on parental rights, when it comes to the emotional wellbeing and beliefs of the children.

Wokeness has allowed a rigid disciplinary standard to slide, to the extent that our young no longer respect their teachers or the school yard rules. The curriculum is delivered in a "kumbaya" manner. For example, in let's say mathematics, rather than teach kids that 2+2=4, teachers are more interested in emphasizing that the students know "why" 2+2=4.

Indeed, the indoctrination of our young is so great, that schools now even conduct climate strikes during school time; at the urging of Greta Thunberg and the climate activists (extinction rebellion). Our youth (also our future voters), are brainwashed into believing that our elected leaders are authorizing the destruction of the planet. I know this first hand.

My son was recently coming first in his senior geography class. When asked to write an essay on the existence of global warming, he refuted the argument, and stated that it was all a hoax. Despite backing up his argument with the facts, he was given a mark of six out of forty, merely because he did not agree with his teachers views on the matter. I was so proud that he stood up for his beliefs and against the indoctrination being delivered.

Argument and debate can be a source of improvement and progress. When you can support your stance through fact, the means to implement new ideologies, can help us all progress as a society. But when your argument is refuted without discussion or acknowledgement of the facts, you are being controlled. It is totalitarian behaviour once again, which stifles development, and which fosters disenchantment within the community.

We need to remember that teachers come and go in the lives of our young children. They are having a major input in the character development of our children, when they are at a most impressionable age. This needs to be countered by parents and immediate family. It is up to mum, dad, grandparents and guardians to instil values, ethical behaviour, character, and morality, in our young.

A failure to address this, will see today's subjective teaching continue to plague future generations. Education has become politicized. But the indoctrination of our youth through their secondary and tertiary education, is unforgivable. Hence the importance of teaching your children yourself, the difference between the left and the right. It is imperative. We have to plan for the future or else capitalism and the freedom it provides is dead. Remember… "a failure to plan is a plan for failure." Or there is the "7P" formula… "Poor Planning and Preparation Produce Piss-Poor Performance."

Governments need to appoint individuals who understand and believe in capitalism, into senior education roles. We have to appoint the right people for the right job. They must be passionate and objective in correcting the current malaise. It is not an overnight fix. The whole system needs revamping from the top down. Rather than a minister for education who is replaced every time a new government is elected, the head of education needs to be there for the long haul, irrespective of whether conservatives or progressives are in power. A sub-committee all conversant with the virtues of capitalism, are then needed to regulate education, at the federal and state level.

Today, too many of the teaching fraternity and education sector, are happy to go with the flow and are not prepared to "unruffle any feathers." The time has come to once again, embrace patriotism and nurture a strong belief in god and country. This can be reinforced through a disciplined delivery of an unbiased re-emphasis on literacy, numeracy, and science. It is not an overnight fix, as re-training and re-educating many teachers in the system, is a case of "too little, too late." It will take years to reproduce a whole new generation of young critical thinkers. Patience with this new doctrine, is better than just the present-day submission into socialist thinking. We have time because socialism also takes years to overwhelm society.

The battle will only get more difficult. Our global village is "bursting at the seams." Consider, that in the year 1800, the world's population was only 1 billion people. Since the turn of the twentieth century the population increased from 1.65 billion to nearly 8 billion today. Rapid population growth only multiplies all the problems facing individuals and nations today. The planet earth is a "finite pie" with limited resources. That now makes for a lot of people each wanting a slice. This can only reduce the slice size, and creates the potential for massive social unrest through huge, further increases in inequality.

Factor in too, that we have recently seen how a health concern in the form of a worldwide pandemic, can destroy economic wellbeing. Consider too, nearly 8 billion people excreting twice daily and urinating 5 or 6 times daily as well. This may one day, come back to haunt us, in terms of creating a "future cesspit for disease" (be it air-borne or water-borne bacteria or viruses).

At the time of writing, the covid-19 virus was being detected in sewerage systems and on animals. How long will it be until the fish of the sea are all contaminated? Same for the meat and food we get off the land. Time for a reset of priorities. There is a whole new industry waiting to be exploited. One that can really save lives. One that is real and not a hoax. One that can create jobs and drive economies to greater heights.

If the activists want something to do, they can busy themselves on solving the problem of how to remove the trillions of face masks, that will soon litter our planet. A more realistic goal than trying to regulate the earth's temperature. Silly buggers!

Afterall, something wiped out the dinosaurs that used to rule the earth. We can leave this one to the scientists, to figure out the best way to protect us from that dilemma in the future. That said, we also cannot allow such unforeseen events to ever be politicized again. Or recognise this when it is happening. We can prepare for the future, but we must also be conscious to fight the fights that currently need fighting.

Some things we can control ourselves. The passing of knowledge to our children. They usually need our guidance until the age of 18. Today's youth seem to know it all, given their comprehensive knowledge of, and obsession with, advanced forms of communication, technology, and information. But it pays to remember, that there is on ongoing quest for power by our elite. They will stop at nothing to in their obsession. They "wouldn't bat an eyelid" about lying to us, the poor constituents and future voters.

Remember that "revenge is a dish, best served cold." We learn from mistakes in relationships. Recognising that narcissists can be hard to live with can be a painful lesson. But it is one that we learn a lot from; to prevent subsequent relationships going the same way. Remember this philosophy, when teaching your children about the difference between left and right, and about having faith in democracy. These are things you can do to protect yourself. Negating narcissism is a blueprint for defeating socialism. Those of the right have learnt to tolerate the socialist progressives. Why can't the left tolerate the conservatives? Why do they carry on "like pork chops?"

Western nations are the envy of other countries, and still with so much untapped potential. Stability, preserved through law and order, and a strong border defence, has stood the test of time. Likewise, our individual and collective wealth, will hopefully, also be preserved by this stability. But this requires respect for our history and a need to maintain traditional values. To not cave into the socialist pressure exerted on society.

As for attempts to erase history by the socialists? Rather than destroy our known history, why don't you, the socialists, get off your backsides, get away from your keyboards, and go out and create your own history? While you are free, you may never get a better chance to fulfil your dreams. You cannot undo the past, but you can determine your own future. Records are made to be broken, not destroyed.

The battle currently playing out before us, is no longer "a little bump in the road" in the grand scheme of things, and need to be viewed with a bit of trepidation. There is a socialist agenda which has unnecessarily distracted us from the real danger. Or is this the deliberate doing of the anarchists and the Chinese?

The Chinese Communist Party has made no secret of the fact that they wish to rule the world. The covid-19 pandemic emanated out of Wuhan. They did nothing to alert the world and prevent its spread. Who is to say, they are not the chief agitators behind the social unrest, playing out in the woke culture wars and BLM protests? Are the anarchists and activists merely the pawns of the socialist puppeteer; China? Are left-wing media outlets, being covertly financed by Chinese sources? It would make sense.

Afterall, the Chinese are buying up assets in foreign nations already. By buying the best farmland, livestock industries, and mineral reserves, the Chinese are smart enough to ensure a source of food for their massive population into the future. Their efforts to buy into communication systems, also gives them strength when it comes to analysing and spying on adversaries. Funny how wokeness is almost non-existent in China. The CCP have no time for cancel culture, freedom of speech, human rights or unlawful behaviour. The West has to wake up and "get with the program."

Maybe over half of the West is already awake to all this. Maybe the general public are smarter than many of our leaders think we are. That is why elections are being won by conservatives. The fact that the Democrats and Labor (socialist progressives), won't denounce recent aggressive Chinese behaviour, is a sign that the socialists are now in bed with Chinese communism. Is this a fourth trojan horse? Was the "Russia hoax," a distraction from the fact that China is trying to influence the future election results? Afterall, the progressives are renowned for their hypocrisy. Remember, "he, who casts the first stone…"

These recent events need to be compared to similar uprisings recorded in the history books. The Western world has witnessed, listened to, endured, and woken up to, significant events most recently. Closed borders have alerted us of the need to protect ourselves first. There is a new sense of patriotism starting to warm the hearts. Self-belief and the need to strengthen our resolve, has not been viewed favourably by the Chinese. Japan awoke the Americans in Pearl Harbour. Has covid-19 alerted the West to the true Chinese intentions? The West never has and never will submit to communism. Will this still be the case in the "nuclear world?"

China can help in all this. What ever happened to transparency? The CCP can ease world suspicions, by inviting the West into Wuhan to fully investigate the virus origins. There is an old saying that remarks "you should not bite the hand that feeds you." The CCP is doing this literally. Maybe they should perhaps instead, seek to understand Western history, rather than impose on us, their communist "garbage."

The CCP need to opt for building up international trust and friendship, and not connivingly, build up mini fortresses on island atolls, upon which, sovereign ownership is debatable. Maybe "Confucius" was really named "Confused," and his true name and preaching's, were lost in translation down the years. Or perhaps, Confucius was a code word for "Confuse the U.S." Do that, distract them, and the world is yours. Scary stuff.

It's funny, but as an evolving species, caught up in a survival of the fittest on this planet, there are only three things that can end the existence of humankind. War, famine, and bacteria (or infection). All three have something in common. China is "rattling its sabre," and flexing its military might. China has nearly 20% of the world's population, who need feeding. China has been the source of the covid-19 pandemic (at the time of writing), and also the origin of similar infectious diseases. CCP exploits can no longer be ignored. Just how much do we value the sanctity of life?

Nothing personal against the Chinese people. I just love their "beef in black bean sauce" and "sizzling Mongolian lamb" dishes. Does this make me a hypocrite too? They are hard-working folk who have the right to exist like the rest of us. Just stop trying to antagonise and control the West. "Or is the CCP a reincarnation of Hitler?" Only time will tell.

As an aside, plagued with the effects of the covid-19 pandemic, the "good old-fashioned burqa," is not a bad option right now, as a defence against the virus, for those of the West. Funny how momentum shifts. Was the virus unleashed on the world by ISIS in a resurgence of their own quest for power? Not much thought has been given to that possibility. Is there collaboration between Muslim and Chinese interests to destroy the West? We are in trouble if this is the case. Is the current state of play, a case of "the enemy of my enemy is my friend?" Hence the rise of socialism and the CCP.

Regardless, the time has come once again, to protect our freedom from the communism that is on the doorstep of every nation in this global village of ours. This almost cyclical battle, is today fraught with danger, as we know the ultimate enemy, is in fact war itself.

Know that local rises in the popularity of socialism, only serve to make the Chinese Communist Party stronger. We should not be handing Australia to the CCP "on a platter." You can help by educating yourself, spreading the word, and teaching your children to learn right from wong… er wrong… er woke… er left. The next chapter in the history of capitalism is waiting to be written. Written by us all.

Don't blindly follow socialism. Do not submit to the woke forces "wrongly" trying to intimidate you. We are all in this together. Be yourself, in a world that is trying to make you something else. This will be your greatest accomplishment.

Epilogue

I cannot believe just how much fun I had writing that. I did not want to stop. Fortunately, the great people at Balboa Press, in their publishing process, have allowed the time for the addition of an epilogue. Given the fluidity of events unfolding around the world, this has allowed the opportunity to further evaluate "what the heck" is happening to the world that we once knew.

Did I say the world was on steroids? Well it's now gone into "roid rage," almost overnight. Time for another book perhaps, but I will try to wrap this up quickly. Consider all that has been discussed in this book. I didn't realise it at the time of writing, but the discussed traits of human behaviour are readily apparent in almost every newsworthy article these days. All our political leaders and the media are displaying the worst of the behaviour.

Of those seven deadly sins, greed is consuming everyone. Technocrats, the elites, and the media have their "snouts in the trough." Money is being made through doing business with the Chinese. Hence the vocal left leaders denouncing those of the right through extensive propaganda. Whether it be, green new deals, free health care, free education, open borders, or an end to racism, know that these are all expensive proposed policies.

If it sounds too good to be true, that is because it is! The Democrats do not care for the blacks in America. They never have and never will. They have weaponised a cohort of the population to serve their need at the pending election. Maybe the youth of America need to read this book too.

Deceit and lying to the American public are the Democratic norm, all virtue of finance accumulated through dealings with China. Look no further than the Wall Street endorsement of Joe Biden in the upcoming American election. It is not hard to see who China want as the next American President. Expect electoral interference and issues with the mail-ballot vote counting.

The elite Democrats are prepared to forego national sovereignty in the selfish pursuit of the mighty dollar. They lie to the masses about the policy promises, merely to secure the votes of the radical lefty socialists. Rest assured, they are not interested in improving the quality of life for the ordinary American. They want their power back. They want the swamp to become murky again to hide their corruption. Gluttony at its unsavoury worst.

Traditional Western values have been under-mined from within by greed. Being blinded by money, has softened the Wests' resolve to stand up; to Chinese intimidation, to wokeness and to the biased left-wing media. It is so hypocritical to do business with the Chinese, and yet ignore the virus unleashed on the world by China. With the exception of Donald Trump, Western leaders seem impotent and oblivious to the threat on our doorstep.

The real battle has been forgotten. It is not between black or white skin colour; it is between socialism and capitalism. The battle between left and right has become surreal, as the West wages war on itself. Consider the following recent developments that exemplify this.

Australian Government officials just admitted on August 13, 2020, that they miscalculated the total area of land decimated by the bushfires of January, 2020. So much for an "unprecedented" catastrophe caused by global warming. "Unprecedented, my arse!"

It seems that the fires were no larger than many other seasonal summer bushfires. Australia has been plagued by them for centuries! Funny that! Officials overstated the amount of burnout land by approximately 24 percent. Only nine-million hectares! It seems that the satellite data doesn't lie. Just to give you an idea, that is an area almost twice the size of Denmark. Feeling stupid now? What about those charity donations and "bushfire relief concerts?"

Where have the so-called "responsible" media disappeared to? They were happy to report the lie and catastrophize the magnitude of the unfolding event, "no questions asked." Are you starting to believe me now, when I say we are being played? Do not let them get away with it. Or were the media just doing their real job, which is lying to us in order to support the narrative? Left-wing media is now a branch of any political party which is in favour of socialism.

Whilst on global warming, Tim Flannery shot to prominence at the turn of the twenty-first century, warning of the dire consequences of global warming, if we didn't change our ways. The lefties fawned over him and put him "front and centre" of their attempts to indoctrinate us; against both, the harmful effects of the sun's rays, and also man's contribution to the pending cataclysmic future facing us all. "The dams will never fill," he proclaimed. "We need to eliminate coal-fired power to save ourselves," he implored. "We need to export our uranium to foreign nations (that were not rich in natural resources), but not use it ourselves." What a lefty lunatic!

Mr Flannery was even anointed "Australian of the Year" in 2007. Can you believe it. Well low and behold, here we are in August, 2020, just a couple of months after the "greatest bushfires of all time," and Australia's biggest dam is about to overflow. Sydney's Warragamba Dam is 99 percent full, and one more day of heavy rain will require the spill gates to be opened. What a goose. And to think that he wanted to fill the atmosphere with sulphur (claim made in May, 2008.) This sulphur was supposed to absorb the sun's rays and thereby save the planet. Just another corrupt scientist trying to make money out of preposterous claims, perhaps? I think he is a mate of Malcolm Turnbull. Say no more.

Apart from the upcoming United States election, the greatest dilemma at present, is the ongoing efforts to combat covid-19. Again, things have played out as my book suggested they might. "Nostradamus, eat your heart out!" It seems that a second wave of the virus has engulfed the entire world. Melbourne was at the centre of Australia's second wave outbreak. Unfortunately, Dan Andrews the lefty Labor State Premier, decided to take the marshalling of quarantine facilities into his own hands. A "captains pick" (something which also led to the downfall of a previous Australian Prime Minister), became the calamity of our times.

"Dan-demic," as he is now affectionately known as, decided in his wisdom, to reject Australian Defence Force (ADF) support. This was offered by the Federal Government, to assist in managing the quarantine facilities in Melbourne. He opted instead, to give the contract to a private security firm (with indigenous links), or in other words, it became a "job for the boys." This was socially and culturally, a better outcome for the local residents.

But as per usual with all things socialist, it has spiralled out of control, with breaches of quarantine, aided and abetted by the engaged security firm. The virus has spread, resulting in many, many deaths. Worse still, is that Melbourne has been forced to enter a stage 4 lockdown. This is crippling the local economy, and has forced border closures across the rest of Australia.

Whilst any death attributed to the virus is tragic, the greatest pain and insult inflicted on the local Victorians, is the Premier's refusal to accept the blame for the calamity. The lefty leader has blatantly lied to the Victorian and the Australian people. He has stated for the record, that Federal ADF support was not offered and certainly not forthcoming. This is despite his own press conferences and written media releases, stating that he has decided to forgo the Federal offers of ADF assistance. Poor Tony Abbott was the victim of a spill against his own Prime-Ministership, for his "captains pick" concerning "the re-introduction of Knights and Dames to the Order of Australia." Another case of duality or "double standards" now emerging between left and right.

The Dan Andrews "captain's pick" is killing hundreds of Australians and financially ruining the economic welfare of thousands more. Where are the media on all this? No one seems willing to ask the hard questions. How do the voters feel? The fact he has not been sacked, is another example of a dictatorship. This totalitarian behaviour is the "end game" of socialism. Are the Melbournians enjoying their freedom? No. He is lying and getting away with it. The media are complicit in ensuring that "the lie becomes the truth." They literally "have blood on their hands too!" Just watch slippery Dan start to apportion the blame onto the Federal Government, in the foreseeable future.

I ask the question; who is more foolish? The fool playing the fool? The fools in the media, who mis-report the lying fool? Or the fools who vote for the fool. Seems to me, that the old chestnut "hypocrisy" is prevalent everywhere. One cannot vote against lefty Labor, when they employ the voter. It is wise "to not bite the hand that feeds you." But what of the economy? It is tanking. It seems that "the People's Republic of Melbourne," has now got what it voted for.

Melbourne is fast becoming a sister-city to Venezuela. A note of caution. In America, people are fleeing lefty-controlled states in droves, apparently "scared out of their minds" for their safety. Current lawlessness, is seeing socialists "on the streets" demanding that they "take" the property of the local residents. That's right, to hell with the law, they just want to take what is not theirs and what hasn't been painstakingly paid for. That's socialism! No ownership, no law, and soon to be no food, medicine, or hope.

Lefty states around Australia and throughout the United States, are virtually bankrupt. But their respective leaders are blaming the virus now for their economic woes. How convenient. Truth is, they were previously economically mis-managed, long before the pandemic. Expect the left-wing media "mob" to now run with this. How many more examples of the "ruination" that socialism causes, do we need?

I will finish with a couple more. I mentioned before, how government spending on aid is easily corrupted. It seems that stimulus payments such as "jobkeeper," are susceptible to similar rorts, with demands that it be offered continuously. These payments hide the real, horrific unemployment figures, but have only served to create more welfare dependency, a "known" socialism "handbrake."

The race for a vaccine against the virus, is being politicized. Poor old Donald Trump could come up with a cure for the virus, but the lefties and the media would refuse to let him announce it. Of that, I am sure. Certainly no "credit where credit is due," likely for that man. The lefties want the virus issues to continue, as they become a vessel for their utopia dream to become a distinct possibility. By destroying the economy, they have leveraged the virus, as a means to get into government, and "attain power."

Now the lefties want compulsory mask wearing. There is no conclusive proof that these are effective. Just as you can't be "half pregnant," the masks are useless, as they only half protect you. The virus is reputedly only transmissible through body orifices. So, a mask over the nose and mouth is ineffective, as it will not prevent the virus entering the body through the ears or eyes. Masks, are the left's equivalent of a Trump "Make America Great Again" cap. They continually urge the wearing of a mask "until they find a replacement for "global warming, or climate change, or BLM, or racism, or…!"

Our leaders have become beholden to the experts. Remember this virus is all about money and power. "Every man and his dog" harbor an opinion and belief about this virus, or have encountered conspiracy theories. But remember the deadly sin "greed." As with most things' government, "throw money at a problem, and the problem only gets bigger." Think about that. It's a virology expert "Christmas" at the moment. The political gift-card that keeps on giving; for all left-leaning government parties trying to get into power or retain government. The rest of us, are just "lambs to the slaughter." The lefty leaders have their eyes on the polls, while us "mere mortals" watch our livelihoods, and quality of life, go "down the gurgler."

I recall mentioning trust, and being careful about what you wish for, when it comes to electing socialist governments. Can you trust socialists to conduct future elections in a trustworthy manner, moving forward?

It certainly no longer appears to be the case in Queensland. The State Parliament currently under lefty Labor rule, has just passed new laws, restricting the budgetary spending of the State opposition Liberal party. Donations towards political candidates are to be capped at $57,000 for Independents, $87,000 for party-endorsed candidates, and $92,000 for party candidates.

However, this will unfairly disadvantage ring-wing candidates, who unlike their left-wing counterparts, do not have the financial backing of multiple unions. This gives the left a massive financial advantage in future election advertising campaigns. See how divisive this "quest for power" has become?

Also, in Queensland, the lefty State Government just passed a law, which prohibits the media from reporting on any political candidate, who is currently before the Crime Corruption Commission and facing allegations of corruption. "Let's change the laws, just to give ourselves a better chance of winning the next election." Quick to realise the idiocy and perceived bias of this measure, the lefty government quickly dissolved this new law, most likely due to the heat they were getting from right-wing media.

The Banana State just happens to be run by lefties, who use inside information on government planning initiatives, to pre-purchase property in areas about to be rezoned. That is, prominent members of the left, are alleged to have been involved in corrupt behaviour. They certainly do not need any further scrutiny.

Financial gain by deception is illegal for most, but not in lefty Queensland. Apparently up there, its ok for you to say "oh, I forgot that my husband just bought a house without telling me." I don't know about you, but if I need a loan for a car or house, it takes weeks of compiling tax returns, proof of earnings and expenditure, and the collating of the value of owned assets, just to get loan approval. Sorry, but its impossible to buy a house and not tell your partner, or accidently forget you just bought a new house. It seems to me that once again, the left-wingers are allowed to connive, lie, and to receive protection from their lefty mates in high places. More duality.

"Go woke, go broke." Queensland, Victoria, South Australia, and the Northern Territory are all the same. Under lefty control, going woke, going broke. The same can be said of a few media enterprises, who have adopted the lefty "woke" stance. In the United States, CNN are suffering from declining audience numbers, as they clutch to the extreme left-wing propaganda and news-worthy stories favouring the left.

Here in Australia, the ABC has lurched so far to the left, that it cannot attract a large audience, and has rapidly become a "basket case." Their current affairs, news, and entertainment shows are riddled with biased, left-wing propaganda. Likewise, any guest with right-wing leanings, is ridiculed and denigrated, and even misquoted to support that dreaded lefty narrative. All at tax-payers expense.

As with most things socialist, the ABC would not last five minutes in the real world. They have become irrelevant, with a left-wing agenda. Perhaps the government is doing us a favour by letting them stay "on the air." In Australia, the ABC is costing more and more to run, while offering less and less, in terms of objective content. At least we can see for ourselves, just how pathetic, living in a socialist society, would be.

Channel nine (free to air television), once the pride of Australia, and 2GB (radio) are also falling into the trap of going "woke," in order to appease the keyboard warriors. Radio stations with woke presenters, are struggling for relevance, and are starting to lose dollars through the loss of advertising revenue. It will be interesting to see how long it is, before they go broke. Their respective ratings are on the slide.

I talked about education that needs fixing, but what about the media? Yes, there are left-wing and right-wing media, but most importantly, we all seek and need the truth from them both. There should be losses of broadcasting licenses for the publication and broadcasting of untruths. We seriously do have to educate ourselves, as to the biased information we are receiving. Many are onto this, but many, many more are oblivious to this fact. Luckily, media outlets are not immune to the "go woke, go broke" phenomenon.

Whilst on media, I just couldn't finish this book without mentioning the recent offering on the ABC's "play school," that last bastion of early childhood education and entertainment. How embarrassing, to have the male host of the show, asking the viewing kiddies "does your daddy or mummy have a beard?" That, from our National Broadcaster (the ABC), which receives billions of dollars in taxpayer funding. It doesn't get any "woker" than that. It's truly embarrassing.

What is the government thinking? But then again, our government has blindly, thrown billions of dollars at the building of nuclear submarines by the French. We are going to retrofit brand-new nuclear subs with diesel engines. This will make the submarines much slower and noisier, and has certainly never been attempted before. (Not to mention the fact they will take 30 years to build). In fact, the submariners who will operate these submarines, if they are ever finished, are not even born yet. Do you see the sheer lunacy of this?

Submarines are designed to be invisible and operate on the basis of stealth. But not down under. True wokeness, also calls for giving your enemy an equal opportunity to kill you. Submarines built properly, are not a "woke weapon of choice," as they give you an advantage. Wokeness will be our downfall and will destroy nations if we are not careful.

The Chinese must be "quaking in their boots." It would also be so easy for the foreign manufacturer, to hide a GPS tracking device in a submarine during construction, so that foreign entities would always know where the sub was. A visible "invisible two-billion-dollar piece of apparatus!" If our government is so reckless in its spending, then why should we care? Looks like socialism is here already. China, it's now over to you! More stupidity. Looks like fiscal responsibility has been "thrown out with the bath water," by the Scott Morrison Government (right).

Do not even start me on the Paris Agreement. Now that "global warming" is somewhat irrelevant, we might as well pull out and save the money. With an economy in ruins, there are better ways to get people and the nation, back on their feet. Afterall, wokeness implies that equality is the goal. If it's good enough for the Chinese to build coal-fired power stations, then we should do the same. At least our electricity costs will diminish. Likewise, the construction of new coal-fired power stations would create ample employment opportunities.

Talk about "killing two birds with one stone." Defund the ABC (instead of the police), abandon the subs program, withdraw from the Paris Agreement, and the government will have billions to spend on re-educating our youth in an objective manner, not to mention spending on the disadvantaged and indigenous populations. Everyone's a winner. But as we see, it's not about that. It is about subverting the masses, to achieve the goal of power. Our new submarines won't save us from an enemy (if the submarines ever arrive, that is), but they will enable a government to hold a seat in Adelaide. See where the priorities really lie?

At the end of the day, we are all free to vote for who we like. That is the beauty of democracy. But if you want to have a life as rich as that which your parents enjoyed, then there is now only one way to vote. Do so wisely. Know that voting left is voting for socialism. Disregard the corrupt left-wing media attempts to play you by appealing to your conscience. The lefty leaders do not care for your welfare, they are using you as their trojan horse, in order to have power to themselves. Know that the freedom you have today, is evaporating before your very eyes. Do not let it disappear.

The media, in their bias, have alienated and divided society. Turn off the television, delete all unnecessary "apps" from your phone, remove yourself from social media platforms, step outside, and open your eyes. See just how beautiful the world is? No racism in sight either. Go and grab life, and do your bit to make the world a better place.

Printed in Australia
AUHW010822281020
336282AU00001B/1

9 781504 322003